ICT in Teacher Development

ICT
in
Teacher Development

Dr. Manoj Kumar Dash
Programme Officer
DEP-SSA, IGNOU
New Delhi.

Foreword

Prof. S.V.S. Chaudhary
Vice Chairperson
National Council for Teacher Education (NCTE)
New Delhi.

NEELKAMAL PUBLICATIONS PVT. LTD.
EDUCATIONAL PUBLISHERS
(EXPORTERS & IMPORTERS)
NEW DELHI HYDERABAD

ICT IN TEACHER DEVELOPMENT

Dr. Manoj Kumar Dash

Foreword

Prof. S.V.S. Chaudhary

First Edition : 2010
Reprint : 2015
(Hardback)

ISBN : 978-81-8316-194-7

NEELKAMAL PUBLICATIONS PVT. LTD.
Sultan Bazar, Hyderabad - 500 095.
✆ 24757140, 24757197, 24757944, Fax: 040-24757951
Delhi Office:
BG5/9B, Paschim Vihar, New Delhi-110 063,
✆ 011-25285894
e-mail : neelkamalbooks@gmail.com
website : www.neelkamalbooks.com

Published by ***Suresh Chandra Sharma*** for ***Neelkamal Publications Pvt. Ltd.*** New Delhi, Hyderabad and printed at ***Sri Vinayaka Art Printers,*** Hyderabad.

Prof. S.V.S. Chaudhary
Vice Chairperson
National Council for
Teacher Education (NCTE)
New Delhi.

Foreword

The Distance Education Programme (DEP) under the *Sarva Shiksha Abhiyan* (SSA), as a national center for open and distance learning activities of the SSA, has been playing a significant role since the inception of the SSA. It has been effectively supporting the initiatives of al the State governments in achieving universalization of elementary education. DEP-SSA is engaged in providing training to elementary school teachers; block/cluster centers coordinators (BRCCs/CRCCs) and other functionaries working in District Institutes of Education and Training (DIETs), State Councils for Education Research and Training (SCERTs), State Institutes of Educational Management and Training (SIEMATs), State Institutes of Educational Technology (SIETs), etc.

Teachers are the backbone of any education system. Training of teachers therefore is the most significant intervention for improving quality of education. Various committees and commissions on education have time and again laid emphasis on the importance of both the pre-service and the in-service teacher education to bring about qualitative improvement in school education across the country. As a consequence, various methods and media are being used to prepare effective teachers. Applications of Information and Communication Technologies (ICTs) have proved their efficacy in imparting high quality education to teachers at various levels. If designed systematically and implemented effectively, ICTs can develop professional competencies in teachers, build their capacity, and facilitate learning of children. Effective implementation of ICTs to train teachers, teacher educators and related functionaries at various levels with quality input is the credo of DEP-SSA.

EduSat, an exclusive communication satellite for education and development, strengthens multipoint communication among educational institutions across the country. It connects all the institutions (known as learning ends) with the teaching ends located at different places in the country. EduSat is aimed at imparting value added education, improving quality of education and training, ensuring availability of excellent content in schools, enriching innovative pedagogy, encouraging change from passive learning to active learning, and providing in-service training to teachers and other functionaries.

A study entitled Information and Communication Technology: Professional Development of Elementary School Teachers was undertaken by Dr. M.K. Dash, Programme Officer (DEP-SSA), Indira Gandhi National Open University to assess effectiveness of satellite-based interactive communication technology for professional development of teachers to accelerate the process of learning of children. The findings of the study are based on data collected from various stakeholders working at the elementary school level.

Dr. Dash critically analyzes the effectiveness of ICTs in general and the potential of EduSat in particular for developing necessary competencies, skills and value system in teachers who in turn would make the teaching learning process more creative, attractive and productive. Various aspects of ICTs including educational needs of elementary school teachers and children as well have been discussed.

The study also reflects the outcome of various interventions made by DEP-SSA in training teachers in different areas, such as content up-gradation, contextual issues and innovations. The findings of the study therefore have implications for all those who are engaged in improving the quality of elementary school education in general and elementary teacher education in particular. The findings presented in this study will be of immense use to teachers, teacher educators, policymakers and research scholars working in the field of school education. The study acquires added importance as more and more institutions are opting for ICT-enabled learning strategies and other features of open and distance learning system. With the expanding acceptability of ICT s for teaching-learning and training, policy planners and administrators have begun to look for ways of blending various methods and media for better results.

I express my sincere appreciation to Dr. Dash for undertaking this research study and publishing it in the form of a book for wider dissemination.

(Prof. SVS Chaudhary)

Preface

Improving the quality of elementary education is one of the major agendas of Government of India. The flagship programme "Sarva Shiksha Abiyan" (SSA) aims at providing useful and meaningful elementary education to all children of 6-14 years age. The framework of SSA emphasizes on the effective implementation of distance education programme for improving professional competencies of teachers on one hand and learning of children on the other. Interventions of distance education programmes supplement to strengthen and sustain the face-to-face mode training and learning to develop knowledge-base, skills, competency and commitment in various functionaries associated wit education of children at elementary level. The role of Information and Communication Technology (ICTs) is very important to ensure the provisions made under SSA related to quality issues. EduSat is the first Indian satellite exclusively meant for educational purpose and for providing connectivity to educational institutions. Launching of EduSat presented a big challenge for optimum utilization of its capabilities to facilitate the pace of progress of our education system. The Government of India has initiated a pilot project in the Sidhi district of Madhya Pradesh for EduSat supported elementary education to utilize EduSat capabilities in strengthening quality elementary education. It focuses on imparting value-based ICT enabled educational programme for improving the quality of education and training both for children and teachers.

The present piece of work is an attempt to assess the effectiveness of ICTs in general and EduSat capabilities in particular for improving the professional development of teachers teaching at elementary school level. The study entitled "Information and Communication Technology: Professional Development of Elementary School Teachers" aims at improving the strategies of implementation of technology-mediated learning to meet the real need of the target group in improving the quality of elementary education. The analysis and interpretation of the result has been made systematically to reflect the efficacy of i) teleconferencing in improving professional development of teachers, ii) EduSat capabilities in accelerating academic achievement of children, quality of transmission of programme, and professional development of teachers. An attempt has been made to collect qualitative data through focus group discussion with i) teachers; ii) block and cluster resource center coordinators; iii) teacher educators; and iv) children and parents as well. Findings of the present study will be useful for implementers and planners in improving the instructional strategies for technology-mediated learning. I am confident that professionals, practitioners, researchers and policymakers will find this book quite informative in the context of planning, designing and implementing various innovative ideas to meet the needs and demands of the target group through ICT- enabled training and learning programmes.

I am highly grateful to Prof. M.L. Koul, Director School of Education, IGNOU for his constant support and guidance for this research study and my deep sense gratitude and thanks goes to Prof. Koul for his contribution in finalizing the document.

I take this opportunity to thank Prof. S.V.S. Chaudhary, Vice-Chairman, NCTE for writing foreword to this work.

The work is the outcome of the blessings and affections of my parents and all family members, who were always the source of my inspiration, motivation, and success. I hope this would serve as a resource document for the professionals associated with effective implementation of technology-mediated learning in the field of education in general and school education in particular.

(Manoj Kumar Dash)

ICT in Teacher Development

Contents

ICT in Teacher Development

Introduction

The pivotal role of education as an instrument of social change by altering the human perspective and transforming the traditional mindset of society is well recognized. Universalization of quality elementary education has become the top priority, especially for developing countries. But the extension of quality education to remote and rural areas has become a Herculean task for a large country like India with multi-lingual and multi-cultural population separated by vast geographical distances and in many instances, inaccessible terrain. Since Independence, there has been a tremendous increase in the number of schools (primary, upper primary, elementary level) as well as enrolment of children. But the lack of infrastructure in rural schools and non-availability of good teachers (professionally trained) is adversely affecting the efforts made in elementary education. The following features characterize the present Indian scenario related to elementary teacher education.

i) Heavy blockage of untrained teachers at elementary level.

ii) Recurrent in-service training of the teachers.

iii) Induction courses for newly recruited teachers to orient in teaching professionals.

iv) Training of large number of para teachers and volunteers working as Education Guarantee Schemes (EGS) or Innovative Alternative Schools.

v) Capacity building/strengthening the Block and cluster level institutions coordinators etc.

Professional training demands, besides acquisition of knowledge, professional skills, positive attitude towards the profession and commitment on the part of the trainers. It is equally true for teaching profession as well. The face-to-face mode of training supported by multimedia for providing curriculum, pedagogical and contextual interventions and reinforcement by evaluative and monitoring mechanism should yield the desired results. The conviction that learning takes place in classroom situation only is no longer valid. ICT has proved that learning is possible any time, and anywhere now. But ICT does not automatically add quality to teaching-learning. Rather its application to the core of teaching can accelerate and improve learning in a number of aspects from basic skills to problem solving, information management, work habits, motivation, lifelong learning habits and the business of education delivery.

It is predicted nowadays that ICT can bring about several benefits to the learner and the teacher. These include;

i) Shared learning resources;

ii) Shared learning spaces;

iii) Promotion of collaborative learning; and

iv) Autonomous learning.

1.1 Characteristic of Technologies

Evaluation of technologies of motion pictures and television during 20th century can be described in terms of media characteristics, delivery systems and communication functions.

1.1.1 Functional Characteristics

These media characteristics are primarily realism or fidelity, mass access, referability and in some cases, immediacy; producers wanted to make persons, places, objects or events more realistic to the viewers. The intent is to ensure that the realistic representation of things or events was as accurate as possible (i.e. fidelity). These characteristics has proven and directed the use of film or television for instructional purposes.

1.1.2 Delivery Systems

Delivery System encompasses both transmission and storage capabilities. The various means whereby the message is sent to the intended audience differ in terms of the breadth of the target group who can access the message. These means of transmission include broadcast television, communication satellite, closed-circuit television, cable access television and microwave relay links.

1.1.3 Storage Media

Television production was often stored in the form of kinescopes. Today, most video programmes are stored on videotape cassette format, which is convenient and is produced in a variety of tape widths. Videotape permits a large number of replays; however, it can deteriorate after excessive use.

1.1.4 Communication Functions

From an instructional point of view, the most important factor in the development of any of these technologies is not the technical aspect of their development but rather the impact of the medium on the target group. Terms that relate to communications functions include instructional television, educational television, mass media, incidental learning, and intentional learning. Instructional television programmes are often transmitted by satellite to school where they are either recorded or used immediately and interactively through a combination of computers and telecommunications.

1.2 Effective Use of Technology

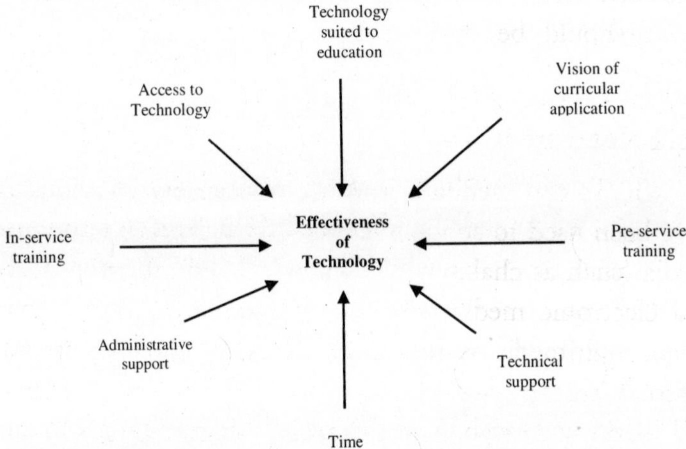

There are many factors on which effectiveness of technology depends. Each and every factor must complement each other for making the use of technology fruitful.

1.3 Information Communication Technologies

Information Communication Technologies (ICTs) have been used in teaching, learning and assessment for many years in distance learning institutions. Today varieties of ICTs, such as audio, video, computers and network technologies are combined to create a multifaceted instructional delivery system. We find a shift in traditional learning led by the teacher to independent learning facilitated by resource-based learning, including utilization of ICTs. It is essential to use it properly for improving learning. We must emphasize on the application/use of ICTs, rather than on ICTs for the sake of it. We need to develop a habit of self-learning and positive attitude towards potentials of various ICT , it can help us in learning effectively and efficiently from those ICTs or other sources of information. There should be explicit objectives in mind before using ICTs.

1.3.1 Need of ICTs

ICTs can facilitate learning of learners. Various ICTs have been used to support learning, which include traditional media (such as chalkboard, textbook, overhead projector etc.) and electronic media (such as computers, interactive audio-video, multimedia system etc.). Technology such as online/ Internet is available 24 hours a day. With the use of Internet and world wide web, a wealth of learning materials in almost every subject can be accessed from anywhere at any time by an unlimited number of learners. Computer and Internet are the tools for learning and developing skills.

1.4 Role of ICTs

ICTs alone do not produce learning; technology is a tool that can be used in many ways, to enhance learning. There are three major categories of instructional use for computer-based technologies; these are: i) learning from technologies; ii) learning about technology; and iii) learning with technology.

Instructional implications of ICTs are mostly based on constructivist theory based on observation and scientific study about how people learn. It holds that people construct their own understanding and knowledge of the world through experiencing things and reflecting on those experiences. Constructivism transforms the student from a passive recipient of information to an active participant in the learning process. Always guided by the teacher, students construct their knowledge actively rather than just mechanically acquiring knowledge from the teacher or the textbook. Students become engaged by applying their existing knowledge and real-world experience -learning to hypothesize, testing their theories and ultimately drawing conclusions from their findings.

Constructivist learning theory suggests that a teacher must understand what learners bring to the learning situation and begin to help students to build their new knowledge. Technology can help to make students' thinking processes more visible to the teacher, something that does not happen when students simply turn in a completed assignment for checking and grading. It is learning with, not from or about, technology that makes computer based technology an important tool in the new paradigm of learning. In order to capitalize on the potential of new technology, and particularly digital technology as a teaching tool, there is an urgent need for the professional development of teachers, to construct professional knowledge about pedagogy, content, and technology, as well as strategies for managing the changing classroom environments brought about with the creation of constructivist learning environments supported by technology. Thus the emerging technologies can provide a platform where different types of media input can converge.

1.5 World of Education and ICTs

The new technologies challenge traditional conceptions of the teaching-learning process and by reconfiguring how teachers and learners gain access to knowledge, have the potential to transform teaching and learning processes. ICTs provide an array of powerful tools that may help in transforming the present isolated, teacher-centered and text-bound classrooms into rich, student-focused, interactive knowledge environments. To meet these challenges, schools must embrace new technologies and appreciate new ICT tools for learning. They must also move towards the goal of transforming the traditional paradigm of learning.

Although schools are embedded in our culture and reflect it values, technological changes that have swept through society have left the education system largely unchanged. In the last two decades a dramatic rift has occurred between the process of teaching and learning in the school and the ways of obtaining knowledge in the society at large. There have been no wholesale revisions of school curricula and no substantial change in the process of teaching. As a result that society and students have become a lot disillusioned with schools. The challenge confronting our educational systems is how to transform the curriculum and teaching-learning process to provide students with the skills to function effectively in this dynamic, information rich, and continuously changing environment.

1.6 Use of Audio Medium

The audio medium has unique characteristics for teaching-learning, which provide realistic experiences such as sounds, places, events etc. It stimulates imagination by presenting the content dramatically. It has a strong impact on learners' thinking, feeling, appreciations, attitudes and motivation. The audio medium is being used in three forms. They are:

i) Audio broadcast;

ii) Recorded audio programmes (cassettes, CD etc.); and

iii) Interactive audio/audio conferencing.

1.7 Use of Video Medium

We remember what we see, more than what we hear. Television generates a sense of belongingness among the learners as it enables the sharing of the same content to thousands of learners. It can reach, teach, motivate and inspire the learners. One could see and hear what is happening at the teaching end. Thus television engages a sense of vision and hearing. It also ensures synchronized sound effects, which create realism as well as imaginative visuals-words composition.

Television is effective for various activities such as role-playing, panel discussion, simulations, demonstrations, lesson practicing, drilling etc. It can provide guided instruction; organize brainstorming sessions and present case studies. Visuals can classify complex ideas, make them easier to understand/remember and provoke emotional responses. Visual medium has certain advantages. The most important among them are:

Motion : Moving images show the events, activities, processes or operations.

Process : Visuals are effective for showing the process of any activity, experiments etc.

Skill Learning : Videocassette is very effective in helping learners acquire skills at their own pace.

Affective Learning : Video programme can be useful in shaping personal and social behavior.

Problem-Solving : Video programme can provide issues, situations or problems to the learners to discuss various ways of dealing with the problem.

Group Learning : Video programme provides a platform for group viewing and group discussion. After the programme, learners can discuss among themselves or with the counselors or with resource persons.

1.8 Use of Teleconferencing

Learning is an active process in which learners construct new ideas, contents on the basis of their existing knowledge and experience. During learning, the learner selects and transforms information, constructs hypotheses and makes decisions. Application of ICTs makes the learning interactive and anticipatory. Teleconferencing is a tool in the hands of teachers and learners to interact in the teaching-learning process and construct their own meaning and share among each other.

Teleconferencing refers to interactive electronic communication among teachers-learners and learners-learners located at more than two places. The concepts of active process and active dialogue come to the fore in teleconferencing. Thus, interactivity has a central role in learning at a distance.

1.9 Types of Teleconferencing

There are three types of teleconferencing based on the content of interactivity for delivery of content and providing learning support. They are: audio conferencing, video conferencing and computer conferencing.

1.9.1 Audio Conferencing

It involves real time exchange of voice information. It is a live, two-way communication, using telephone lines or satellite, connecting learners at different locations. Both the teachers and the learners can hear each other's views/ experiences. All the learners get the same learning input and interactivity. They, however, cannot see the presentation, demonstration or experiment. Interactive Radio Counseling (IRC) allows learners to participate in a presentation in real time, and allows for a highly interactive, synchronous learning environment.

1.9.2 Video Conferencing

It allows exchange of voice and visuals. It allows two or more learners, located at different places, to participate in the teaching-learning process. There are two types of video conferencing.

- One-way video and two-way audio conferencing.
- Two-way audio and two-way video conferencing.

1.9.3 Computer Conferencing

It allows exchange of information with the support of multimedia through computers. In other words it requires the use of computer with a browser. This helps in exchanging audio, video and graphics via Internet. Interaction through computer conferencing can be both synchronous and asynchronous.

1.10 Computer-Enabled Learning (CEL)

In computer-enabled learning, the computer is the primary medium of teaching and learning. It offers interactive environment in which one can interact with the computer as learning materials are stored on the personal computer.

Web-based learning provides integrated environments of various technologies to support diverse needs of the learners via the Internet. It is self-paced, highly interactive, results in increased retention rates and has reduced costs. Internet-based services and software provide a synchronous learning environment in which one has access to text-chart, web-conferencing, audio and video files and more. This technology can enable to share documents and applications with other users.

Computer conferencing connects two or more computers together to conduct information exchange. The learning materials delivered through a variety of ways include readings, handouts, audio-video components and traditional lectures. There is interactivity with the learners group. Computer conferencing allows communicating on topics of mutual interest. The necessary software is hosted on a multi-user computer system, which has sufficient disc space to store and retrieve all messages/information that are written. Computer conferencing create a virtual- classroom for formal and informal contact between fellow learners and experts. One can use computer conferencing at almost any time, from anywhere and at one's own pace. The time may be mutually decided in consultation with the expert and fellow learners. There is freedom to interact on the topic of mutual interest with the expert.

ICTs have the potential to provide quality educational inputs. These bring inaccessible resources to the user at the learning centre, home or workplace. ICTs offer flexibility to learn from anywhere, at any time and at users own pace. Use of ICT can bridge the gap of time and space in learning at a distance with quality input. In order to learn from ICTs, the learner should be motivated enough and have a favorable attitude towards learning from ICTs. Beside, the learner has to take active part in the ICT-enabled learning processes.

1.11 Introduction to Educational Satellite

Satellite can establish the connectivity between urban educational institutions with adequate infrastructure imparting quality education and the large number of rural and semi-urban educational institutions that lack the necessary infrastructure. Besides supporting formal education, a satellite system can facilitate the dissemination of knowledge to the rural and remote population, about important aspects and allow professionals to update their knowledge base as well. Thus, in spite of limited trained and skilled teachers, the aspirations of the growing student population at all levels can be met through the concept of tele-education.

The concept of beaming educational programmes through satellites was effectively demonstrated for the first time in India in 1975-76 through the Satellite Instructional television Experiment (SITE) conducted using the American Application Technology Satellite. In 1983, a variety of educational Development Communications Project and Training and Developmental Communication Channel further demonstrated the efficacy of tele-education. With the success of the INSAT-based educational services, a need was felt to launch a satellite dedicated for educational service and ISRO conceived the EduSat Project in October 2002.

EduSat is the first exclusive Satellite for serving the educational sector. It is specially configured to meet the growing demand for an interactive satellite-based distance education system for the country through audio-video medium, employing Direct to Home (DTH) quality broadcast. The satellite will have multiple regional beams covering different parts of India -five Ku-Band transponders with spot beams covering northern, northeastern, eastern, southern and western regions of the country; a Ku-band transponder has its footprint covering the Indian mainland region and six C-band transponders with their footprints covering the entire country.

EduSat the first Indian satellite strongly reflects India's commitment to use space technology for national development, especially for the development of the population in remote and rural locations. With the launch of EduSat on 20 September 2004, enormous capacity for providing quality education at the national, regional and state levels has become possible. EduSat provides connectivity across the country irrespective of the location of the school or the learner. It has the capacity to create virtual classroom, provide on-demand audio-video programmes, transfer date/ text through the network, and facilitate interactivity in the teaching-learning process. The connectivity could be both-ways audio, one-way video and two-way audio or both ways video.

For data access learning/teaching material could be made available in central database that children and teachers could access as and when required. Audio networks could be established for organizing audio conferences. Thus, the emerging techniques can provide a platform where different types of media input can coverage.

1.12 Project on EduSat for Hindi Speaking States

The Department of Space, Government of India, has made heavy investment on launch of EduSat on September 20, 2004, a dedicated satellite for education and development. The services of the satellite are available 24 hours. The Dept. of Space, Govt. of India has activated one National Hub to support national level networks and activate five regional hubs to support regional/state level networks for interactive multicast and online modes of communication for educational purposes in different regions/states. In the present project, it was intended to develop district level networks with initial focus on classroom-based learning, teachers training, literacy and development of knowledge repositories, as effective and sustainable sources courseware. The district network connects more than 62 schools, District Institutes of Education and Training (DIETs), Block Resource Centers (BRCs), and Cluster Resource Centers (CRCs) to meet district level requirements for education and training of teachers and schoolchildren.

Though physical facilitators for universalization of elementary education exists to a very large extent in all the states and inspite of the efforts and initiatives taken in this connection, a lot is required to be done to improve the quality of education especially at the elementary school level. One of the reasons for this is the difficulty to reach most of the locations where primary/elementary schools are situated; poor communication and infrastructure facilities do not allow us to develop any continuous system of providing additional inputs to both the children and teachers, for improving the quality of education. It is expected that the extensive reach of satellite communication will enable us to address some of the major issues like professional development of teachers for quality elementary education to ensure universal access to quality education at primary/elementary level. In general, the Hindi speaking states like Bihar, Chhatisgarh, Jharkhand, Madhya Pradesh, Rajasthan and Uttar Pradesh have perhaps remained less developed because of poor quality of education and its limited access. However, here is a major advantage in all these states: Hindi is a common link language for teaching-learning process especially in the primary/ elementary schools to facilitate sharing of content and other resources ensuring fairly wide expansion and extensive reach at relatively low costs.

The objective of this project is to develop value-added ICT enabled educational software and its dissemination for improving the quality of education/training both for children and teachers and support literacy and adult education programmes. However, before this extensive project is launched in the entire Hindi speaking region, it is considered necessary to begin with a pilot project by selecting one of the least developed districts in one of the states in the region with greater focus and a few other locations in the adjoining districts of other states. It is in this background that for a meeting of MHRD-ISRO-IGNOU, the Sidhi district of Madhya Pradesh was chosen for main focus with a total of nearly 350 Receive only terminals and 12 Satellite Interactive Terminals supported by EduSat. Out of these, a few terminals in the schools of adjoining districts of other states were also connected on priority basis. It is with this purpose that the Department of Space, MHRD and District Education Council/IGNOU have agreed to jointly work on the pilot project in collaboration with the School Education department of Madhya Pradesh.

1.13 Challenge to Educational Technology Community

Community of Educational Technology faces five main challenges i.e.

- Transcend the constraints and limits of the means and methods of instructional technology.
- Understand the difference between the design of education as a social system and instructional design.
- Develop open-systems and competence in systems design.
- Create programmes and resources that enable our educational community to develop systems and competence in system design.
- Assist our communities across the nation to engage in the design and development of their systems of learning and human development.

❖ ❖ ❖

Context of the Study

CHAPTER 2

2.1 Pilot Project (for Hindi Speaking States)

Sidhi is in educationally backward district in comparison to other districts such as Indore and Bhopal in the state of Madhya Pradesh. It is dominated by rural area/ population. Sidhi district comprises of 8 Blocks, 149 cluster resource centers and 1753 villages. Overall the literacy in the district is 52.80 percent, which is much lower than the literacy level of Indore and Bhopal districts. In Indore the literacy rate is 74.80 percent and in Bhopal it is 75.10 percent. The female literacy in Sidhi district is very low i.e. 36.40 percent; this is also very low in comparison to all these districts.

To provide easy access to all children of 6-14 years age group in this district, there are 1455 Education Guarantee Scheme/Alternative Schooling Centers. As of date (2003), there are 22.80 percent single teacher primary schools in the district, which is also very high in the Sidhi district in comparison to Indore (10.30 percent) and Bhopal (13.00 per cent) districts. There is less number of urban schools in Sidhi. Majority of the schools in the district are being financed and managed by the State Government. There are 3187 primary and 988 upper primary schools in the district of Sidhi with enrolment of approximately 141.78 lakh children

(76.48 lakhs boys and 65.30 lakhs girls) enrolled in class I to VIII in the state. There are still 4.28 lakhs children in the age group of 6-14 years who are out of school. The actual achievement in terms of retention in schools up to class VIII is still problematic in the state. The dropout rate at primary and elementary school level in M.P. is 21.4 and 21.5 per cent respectively. For class beyond VIII and up to XII, the dropout is even more problematic Similar is the situation in some other neighboring Hindi speaking states. The major factor for such an abnormal dropout rate seems to be the poor quality of education and a very weak and inadequate system of teacher education. The later results in adversely affecting the capabilities of elementary schoolteachers and hence the quality of learning at elementary school.

The teacher educators in training institutions in the states, such as DIET, BRCs, CRCs, have some experience and expertise in use of educational aids including computers. They however need further motivation and up-gradation of knowledge and skills to act as master trainers for effective training of teacher through ICT supported networks, so that they can help the schoolteachers to impart quality education and improve classroom transaction.

2.2 Objectives of the Project

EduSat networks with extensive reach and connectivity can effectively empower teachers and improve quality of elementary education in the majority of schools in district of Sidhi and a few other schools in adjoining districts of other states. The objectives of this project were to:

i) Ensure availability of quality content online and through variety of access devices in schools.

ii) Enrich existing curriculum and pedagogy at different levels by employing all the technologies available, through the EduSat including virtual classrooms, video on demands etc.

iii) Promote a shift from current passive learning based on instructors to active learning.

iv) Support to total literacy/adult education and compulsory education for all in the age group of 6-14 years.

v) In-service and recurrent training of schoolteachers; continues up-gradation of their knowledge and skills.

vi) Create an enabling environment for the optimal use of the EduSat in providing teacher training.

vii) Training of teachers and master trainers in handling of IT supported and ICT-enabled education through EduSat and

viii) Ensuring inclusive integrated education for the differently-abled.

One of the greatest advantages of EduSat supported networks, due to their fast and extensive reach is to provide access to some of the best teachers and teaching processes for a very large target group of learners. This will significantly enhance the quality of education. Thus, majority of the schools, BRCs and CRCs located in different parts of the district were connected with EduSat network. A few locations in adjoining districts of neighboring Hindi speaking states were also connected for the project.

2.3 Network Provided by ISRO

The following network was provided by IGNOU for wider dissemination in the Sidhi district and its neighboring districts of other states.

i) 700 Receive Only Terminals (ROTs) Sidhi District.

ii) 150 ROTs (50 each in the three adjoining districts of other states)

iii) 9 Satellite Interactive Terminals (SITs) in Sidhi for Teacher Training (8 BRCs and DIET).

iv) 3 SITs (one each in three adjoining districts of other states)

v) One Hub to support the network at Prantiya Shisha Mahavidyalaya, Jabalpur.

The following table gives detailed description of the distribution of ROTs and SITs

Table-2.1: Distribution of ROTs and SITs

S.No.	*State*	*District*	*No. of ROTs*	*No. of SITs*
1	M.P.	Sidhi	700	9
2	Chhattisgarh	Koria	50	1
3	U.P.	Sonebhadra	50	1
4	Bihar	Vaishali	50	1
TOTAL			850	12

The Hon'ble HRD Minister has formally inaugurated the pilot project on Dec. 17, 2005 from EMPC, IGNOU, New Delhi. The Hub (teaching end) for transmission through EduSat at PSM, Jabalpur and SIT at DIET, Sidhi were inaugurated on the same day.

2.4 Orientation of Teachers

DEP-SSA, IGNOU has organized ten orientation programmes for the elementary schoolteachers on utilization of EduSat capabilities during September 2005 to March

2006. These orientation programmes were organized in collaboration with Regional Centre, IGNOU, Jabalpur, Rajya Shiksha Kendra, Bhopal and State Project Offices of Bihar, Chhatisgarh and Uttar Pradesh. Details of schedule and number of participants of orientation programmes are given in table 2.2

Table-2.2: Details of Orientation Programmes

S. No.	*Duration*	*Venue*	*No. of Participants*
1	Sept. 26-28, 2005	PSM, Jabalpur, M.P.	96
2	Nov. 05-07, 2005	DIET, Sidhi M.P. BRC, Waidhan	72 81
3	Nov. 16-18, 2005	DIET, Sidhi BRC Waidhan	84 104
4	Nov. 19-26, 2005	DITE Sidhi BRC Waidhan	129 152
5	Feb. 27 – March 01, 2006	BRC, Baikunthapur Chhatisgarh	50
6	March 06-08, 2006	DIET, Robertganj	49
7	March 31-April 02, 2006	Diet, Vaishali, Bihar	51
		TOTAL	**868**

The main objective of the orientation programme was to orient teachers in teaching through EduSat and their role responsibility in facilitating children's learning i.e. to make them prepare for tele-teaching and how to act as an ideal facilitator during transmission through EduSat. Besides this, certain topics, which were covered during the orientation, are

i) ICT-enabled and ICT-supported education on the concept and need.

ii) EduSat: its characteristics and capabilities.

iii) Project implementation, monitoring and feedback.

iv) Role and responsibilities of teachers in the project.

v) Designing of tele material, tele teaching.

vi) Learning from interactive multimedia CDs and concept of collaborative education.

A group of 50 teachers were selected for intensive training in teaching (live) thorough EduSat. Teachers were trained on the development of e-content and its presentation through television (studio presentation).

Since December 19, 2005, teaching through EduSat is being carried out from 11:00 to 01:00 p.m. (repeated from 02:00 p.m. to 04:00 p.m.). Elementary schoolteachers from the Sidhi district and Jabalpur were invited to teach the hard spots identified by state authorities. Besides teaching elementary classes, one hour (11:00 a.m. to 12:00 p.m.) transmission on every Saturday is being used for teacher education to provide training/orientation to primary and elementary schoolteachers exclusively.

Although EduSat is used as a medium for the training/ education of teachers, it raises several questions with regard to professional development of teachers for quality elementary education.

2.5 Research Questions

The study aims to answer the following

i) Do the teachers have favorable perceptions towards teaching through EduSat in relation to; i) acceptance of technology; ii) readiness to use technology; iii) access, feasibility and viability; iv) teaching–learning process adopted in the technology; v) interaction pattern both at learning and teaching end; vi) adequacy of content coverage; vii) presentation style including use of language and TLM; and viii) communication skill?

ii) Does the teaching through EduSat help in professional development of teachers in relation to; i) improvement of subject matter; ii) teaching-learning technique; iii) classroom management; iv) understanding group behaviour; and v) modification of teaching behaviour?

iii) Does the teacher face any problem (academic and administrative) during teaching and learning through EduSat?

iv) How can EduSat programme be made more effective for providing quality elementary education?

2.6 Statement of the Problem

A STUDY ON THE EFFECTIVENESS OF INFORMATION AND COMMUNICATION TECHNOLOGY: PROFESSIONAL DEVELOPMENT OF ELEMENTARY SCHOOL TEACHERS

2.7 Objectives of the Study

The following objectives have been set forth for the present study.

- To study the effectiveness of technology (teleconferencing) on professional development of teachers.
- To study the effectiveness of EDUSAT on the academic achievement of children at primary grade.

- To study the perception of teachers and other functionaries on teaching and learning through EDUSAT
- To study the effectiveness of EDUSAT in the professional development of teachers.
- To suggest measures for further improvement of transmission through EDUSAT.

2.8 Definition of Key Terms

2.8.1 Professional Efficiency

Teaching is a complex task and teachers and other educators need substantial time to test new ideas, assess their effects, adjust their strategies and approaches and assess these again to reach all students and make learning meaningful to them.

Professional development can no longer be viewed as single event that occurs on a particular day of the school year; rather it must become part of the daily work life of educators. Teachers, administrators and other school system employees need time to work in study groups, conduct action research, participate in seminars, coach one another, plan lessons together, and meet for other purpose. Fine (1994) states, "School change is the result of both individual and organizational development." When professional development is viewed as a central component of teaching, most decisions and plans related to embedding professional development in the daily work life of teachers will be made at the local school level. Some reformers have recommended that at least 50 percent of teacher's work time should be devoted to professional study and collaborative work.

This time must be part of virtually every school day and must be closely linked to the day-to-day demands of teaching (e.g. collaborative lesson planning, assessment of students' work). Schools must provide time for professional development as an integral part of teachers' professional life. The National Education Association (1994) recommends that 50 percent of teacher's time be given to professional development. Although providing even 20 percent of teacher's work time for these activities may seem like an unachievable goal, the school system needs to strive for it by "thinking outside the box" to revamp the working conditions of teachers so that they have the necessary support within the school system so necessary for planning, and implementing ambitious reforms.

This explains why it is essential to develop professional efficiency of teachers and other functionaries through various distance learning activities, with a view to maximize their potentiality to achieve the target of quality elementary education. EduSat is one of the crucial modes used for this end.

2.8.2 Effectiveness

Effectiveness means, "producing a desired or intended result according to a pre-determined goal". The result must be explicit and available for service so as to meet the individual and society. So every teaching activity should be directed towards effective attainment of a planned outcome.

2.8.3 Criteria of Developing Effectiveness

Effectiveness is an important aspect of achieving perfection in any field. There are various strategies, which can help an individual develop/achieve effectiveness in one's area. There are as follows

- Alleviate one's anxiety significantly to improve one's daily functioning.
- Undertake activity according to capability.
- Experience the satisfaction of a job well done and positive achievement.
- Overcome personnel, social and professional obstacles and challenges, if any through sustained goal-directed efforts.
- Limit yourself to success-oriented goals.
- Identify and build on your fundamental character, strengths and abilities;
- Mange your stress and time effectively.
- Focus on and heighten your motivation for goals and overcome procrastination.
- Try to become more efficient while at work or play.
- Create a favorable image of yourself that commands respect from colleagues.
- Try to communicate more persuasively in any situation;
- Promote yourself comfortably without selling; and
- Control your emotions and your thinking to work in a cool manner for achieving goals and avoid against them.

2.8.4 Information Communication Technology (ICT)

Technology has dramatically penetrated into every area of society and every aspect of our social and cultural lives. Television rediscovered and recast the world as a direct experience. Computer made it possible for vast amount of information to be made instantly available and processes with a key. The very nature of work has changed, with an increasing demand for workers who can master new technologies and use them. Children are now used to environments where they can control information flow and access it, in which geographical mobility, intellectual flexibility and synthesis of work and learning are the norms.

New technologies challenge traditional conceptions of both teaching and learning and, by reinforcing how teachers and learners gain access to knowledge, have the potential to transform the teaching and learning processes. ICTs provide an array of powerful tools that may help in transforming the present isolated, teacher-centered and text- bound classrooms into rich, student-centered, interactive knowledge-based environment.

To meet these challenges, our teachers must embrace new technologies and appreciate new ICT tools for learning and training. They must also move towards the goal of transforming the traditional paradigm of learning. Thus, the emerging technologies can provide a platform where different types of media inputs namely; i) audio medium; ii) visual medium; iii) teleconferencing; and iv) computer education and e-learning etc. can be covered

Situational analysis of the use of ICTs suggests that there is a vast scope of their applications in teacher education programmes more specifically at the lower and upper primary stages. Being a formative stage of children, for the children of age group 6-14 years, it demands a better quality of educating, which could be ensured by better qualified, well-trained and unlighted-teachers. ITCs are best suited to meet this imperative demand. On the basis of the earlier experiments, it is learnt that providing adequate inputs can ensure optimal utilization of these ICTs for teacher education programmes. It needs planning, organization and institutional structure for ensuring user-responsiveness; content generation suitable to local specific needs in regional languages is the prerequisite for effectiveness of ICTs. Besides this, there is a need to train, empower and motivate teachers and children. Regular monitoring of the use of different components of ICT and remedial strategies can also ensure quality of effectiveness of technologies.

2.8.5 EDUSAT: Milestone in Development of Communication Networks for Education

EduSat is the first Indian satellite designed and developed for serving the educational sector. It is mainly intended to meet the demand for in interactive satellite-based distance education system for the country. It strongly reflects India's commitment to use space technology for national development, especially for the development of the population in remote and rural locations. It is a collaborative project of MHRD and ISRO, Govt. of India.

The launch of EduSat marks a major milestone in the country and posseses enormous challenges as well as offers excellent potential for quality education. It was proposed by MHRD, Govt. of India to use the ICT capabilities of EduSat satellite for elementary education, literacy, vocational training and teachers' training. It is the first exclusive satellite for serving the educational sector. It is especially configured for audio-visual medium, employing digital interactive classroom and multimedia, multi-centric system. The satellite has multiple regional beams covering different parts of India. Extensive teaching-learning using these networks has been growing fast.

2.9 Rationale of the Study

In the past several studies have been conducted to study the effectiveness of ICTs. Evaluation of a study on ICT (teleconferencing) in non-formal education indicates that the viewers find the programme interesting and practically useful in their day-to-day activities. Viewers opined that the programme helped them to: i) improve their knowledge (55 percent); ii) spend their leisure profitably (41 percent); and iii) find opportunity for self-employment (24 percent) (Jayatillike, B.G. 2001). Interactive communication using satellite and long distance telephone links contributed to the knowledge gain of the participants and conceptual understanding of participants improved significantly (Trivedi, 1998). Perceptions and reactions towards using teleconferencing as a mode of instruction were generally favourable; participants clarified that regular use of teleconferencing in future would depend upon improvement in timing, access to telephonic facilities, and high quality of programme content. There are usually complaints about inadequate reaction time, long holding time before a call would mature, poor quality of audio in the telephone call and echo caused by not muting the television set when questions are asked (Reddi, 1996).

Means and Olson (1997) found that technology can support teacher's efforts to engage students in long-term, complex projects by dramatically enhancing student motivation and self-esteem, making obvious need for longer blocks of time, creating a multiplicity of roles, teaching to student's specialization in different aspects of technology use, encouraging greater collaboration, and giving teachers additional impetus to take on a coaching or an advisory role. It is expected to transform teachers already in service into an empowered teaching force. This can be possible by developing confidence through personal knowledge acquired, the ability to make decisions and to take appropriate action based on necessary facts. These are considered to be the characteristics of an empowered teacher (Mohanty, 2001). Empowering teachers is the ultimate objective of accelerating the process of empowering children as learners. (Berkdale – Ladd, 1994). With rapid improvement in the area of communication, a new social pattern has been created and need for an approach to learning in contrast to the traditional one can be seen. (Rajasingham, 1995) with ICT providing new avenues of access to resources and people at all times; it has tremendous potential to facilitate teachers' learning and professional development (Maier, 1998). The best prediction of skills that teacher education graduates have is infusing Information and Communication Technology (ICT) into instruction. (Radha Mohan, 2004). Freedmon (1989) conducted a study to examine the use of computer graphics among boys and girls and observed that fifth grade girls were more concerned than were boys with using color, color combination and relationships among object shapes. Boys were more interested in movement, and sometimes conceptualized shapes as subjects capable of violence.

No study has been conducted so far to find out the effectiveness of EDUSAT on professional competency/ development of teachers. So, in the present context, it was felt essential to study the effectiveness of EDUSAT with regard to professional development of elementary schoolteachers. EDUSAT is one of the emerging technologies in the field of ICT and is being used in the field of elementary education for providing quality teaching-learning input. Professional development of teacher is one of the prime concerns of EDUSAT network. Hence, it was decided to undertake this study exclusively with regard to professional development of teachers.

2.10 Delimitation of Study

The scope of the study has been limited to its area, method, sampling, tools and techniques of the study. The study has been delimited in the following ways.

- The study is confined to professional development of elementary schoolteachers through EduSat only.
- The study has been conducted in one district of the state of Madhya Pradesh i.e. Sidhi District.
- The study has been conducted on 80 teachers belonging to 8 different blocks of Sidhi district (i.e. 10 teachers have been taken from each block). 8 BRC coordinators (i.e. one from each block) and teacher rducators from Sidhi DIET.
- A questionnaire on five different areas of professional development and another questionnaire on various aspects of transmission through EduSat have been taken into consideration for assessing the perception of teachers on the effectiveness of EduSat.
- A focus group discussion organized at Sidhi DIET where two teachers from eight different blocks, Block Resource Centre Coordinator of each block and five teacher educator from Sidhi DIET were invited to elicit questionnaire responses from them regarding their perception and other stakeholders towards EduSat is an important tool of ICTs.
- The sample of the study was drawn from Sidhi district of Madhya Pradesh only.

- A descriptive Survey Method has been used in the present study.
- Statistical techniques like percentage and Chi-Square test were employed to analyze the data.

Review of Related Literature

The review of the research literature pertaining to the problem of study becomes essential for the researcher in order to have complete and thorough information of the work done in his country and abroad. The area of professional development of elementary schoolteacher through EDUSAT is a new field of study in the country.

In the present study the investigator has collected most of the relevant and reported studies done in the field of professional development of teachers through information communication technologies related to the field. The present chapter provides a thumbnail account of such studies, and their outcomes. The available studies, which have direct or indirect bearing upon the present study, have been presented.

3.1 Studies Related to the Present Study

Vygolsky (1962) found that in shared learning resources the students and teachers enjoy the facility of shared information wherever they are in school through television monitor. In shared learning spaces, networked computing facilities create a distributed environment where learners can share workspaces, communicate with each other and their teachers in text form and access a wide variety of resources from internal and external database via web-based systems. Using these shared systems, students develop transferable skills, simultaneously acquiring knowledge of other cultures, language and traditions. Furthermore, students are able to make links between Internet thinking and external social interaction via the keyboard to improve their social and the intellectual development in the best constructivist tradition.

Cradler (1972) found that technology alone does not have a significant impact on teaching and learning. Technology is a tool when used with tested instructional practices and curriculum can be an effective catalyst for educational reform.

Alwitt et al (1980) revealed that certain audio-effects were effective in gaining attention from non-viewing children. These included auditory changes, sound effects, laughter, instrumental music, and children's women and peculiar voices. They concluded that auditory devices cured the children and that an important change was taking place in the programme, which might be of interest, thereby promoting attention. It is also concluded that audio effects do not appear to have any significant effect before the age of 24 to 30 months. An attribute (feature) comes to have a positive or negative relationship to attention; we hypothesize, based on the degree to which it predicts relevant and comprehensive content. A child can thus use an attribute to divide attention between TV viewing and other activities. Full attention is given when an attribute is predictive of understandable content and terminated when an attribute predicts irrelevant boring and incomprehensible content.

Anderson and Field (1983) explain that formal features perform two significant functions. First, they mark the beginning of important content segments, and second, they communicate producer-intended concepts of time, space, action and character. The formal features, which comprise such television effects as montage, are able to convey changes in time, place, or movement integral to a viewer's ability to comprehend story content and plot as well as simply to gain or hold attention. It is in the area of comprehension that formal features appear to play the most important role.

Ong and Health (1983) methodically experiments on 12-years old children and found no differences in brain wave activity between projected text and text presented on the television screen. But differences were found between text presented on the television screen and documentary or interview programming, whereas no differences were found between the two type of programming. Both the text and interview programme produced right and left hemisphere effects, while the documentary alone resulted in greater right hemisphere activity.

Bowse (1986) reviewed research on learning from films and concluded that i) films are effective in teaching inquiry learning and problem solving; ii) unstructured films are more effective for teaching problem solving; iii) films are effective in teaching observation skills and attention to detail; iv) low-aptitude students tend to benefit more from films; v) films tend to be more effective for field independent students; and vi) films can positively influence self-concept.

Newman, (1990) reported another factor influencing the impact of technology on student achievement in that changes in classroom technologies correlate to changes in other educational factor as well. Originally, the determination of student achievement was based on traditional methods of social scientific investigation; it asked whether there was a specific causal relationship between one thing –technology and another student achievement. Because schools are complex, social environments, however, it is impossible to change just one thing at a time.

Sprafkin, Gadow and Abelman (1992) describe the research on television on three distinct chronological phases: i) medium-orientation phase; ii) child-orientation phase; and iii) interaction phase. In medium-oriented phase television was seen as a powerful instructional tool that required research to describe its effectiveness. In child-orientation phase focused on the relationship of television to young viewers, individual characteristics and aptitudes. In interaction phase, effects of television were seen as complex three-way interaction between characteristics of medium (such as type of content), the child viewer variables (such as age) and factors in the viewing environment (such as parents and teachers).

Vockell and Schwartz (1992) suggest that computer-assisted instruction can increase achievement because it leads to automatic lower-level skills through extended practice. A computer that is endlessly patient with the learner monitors this practice. In the tutorial form of commuter-assisted instruction, the computer provides additional information to the learner if an incorrect answer is supplied. This continues until the learner is successful.

Bruer (1993) notes that research overwhelmingly concentrates on weakness of poor children. Very little research has been done on their strength. In addition, the weaknesses identified are often deficiencies in terms of the traditional organization and content of schooling. Very little thought has been given to the idea of changing schooling to accommodate new kinds of students; all efforts have been devoted to changing students so that they can fit into the school. The technology of mass education is quite adept at "breaking knowledge and skills into thousands of little standardized, de-contextualized pieces which could be taught and tested one at a time.

Honey (1993) conducted a study on communication technology and found that i) science, social awareness and cultural exchange projects are perceived to be the most effective telecommunication activities to do with student; and ii) the most highly rated incentives for using telecommunications with students included expanded students awareness about the world, accessing information that would otherwise be difficult to obtain, and increasing students inquiry-based and analytical skills. With regard to educators' outcome, Honey found:

- More than two-third of the educators report that integrating telecommunications into their teaching has made a real difference to how they teach.
- Conducting telecommunication activities with students enables teachers to spend more time with individual students, less time with lecturing to the whole class, and allows students to carry out more independent work.

Becker (1994) indicated that it is important to build time into the daily schedule allowing teachers time to collaborate and to work with their students. Engaged learning through technology is best supported by changes in the structure of the school day, including longer class period and more allowance for team teaching and interdisciplinary work. For example, when students are working on long-term research projects for which they are making use of online resources (such as artwork, scientific data sets, or historical documents), they may need more than a daily 30-or 40 minutes period to find, explore and synthesize these materials for their research. As schools continue to acquire more technology for student use and as teachers are able to find more ways to incorporate technology into their instruction, the problem will no longer be not enough computers but not enough time.

Sahoo (1994) found that participants were positive on the role of teleconferencing and responded positively and quality of presentation of all programmes was found to be either of average or high standards. Quality of presenter/ experts was rated high. The time provided for reinforcement and other immediate follow up with learners was found to be average

West Laboratory (1994) conducted a review of current research and evaluation finding from various studies has determined that the integration of technology and telecommunication into education i) increases performance when interactivity is prominent; ii) increases opportunities for interactivity with instructional programmes; iii) is more effective with multiple technologies; iv) improves attitude and confidence – especially for at risk students; v) provides instructional opportunities otherwise not available; vi) can increase opportunities for student-constructed learning; vii) increases student collaboration on projects; viii) increases mastery of vocational and workforce skills; ix) helps prepare students for work when emphasized as a problem solving tool; x) significantly improves students problem-solving skills; and xi) increases the preparation of students for most careers and vocations.

For the professional development of teachers, he pointed the following strategies to be adopted by the classroom teachers i.e.

i) Determine the purpose of using technology in the classroom as determined by the specified educational goals. It is used to support inquiry, enhance communication, extend access to resources, guide students to analyze the visualized data, enable product development, or encourage expression of ideas. After the purpose is determined, select the appropriate technology and develop the curricula. Create a plan for evaluating students work and assessing the input of technology;

ii) Coordinate technology implementation efforts with core learning goals, such as improving students' writing skill, reading comprehension, mathematical reasoning and problem-solving skills;

iii) Collaborate with colleagues to design curricula that involve students in meaningful learning activities in which technology is used for research, data analysis, synthesis and communication;

iv) Promote the use of learning circles, which offer opportunities for students to exchange ideas with other students, teachers, and professionals across the world.

v) Create opportunity for students to share their work publicly, through performance, public service, open house, science fairs and videos; use the occasion to inform parents and community members about the kinds of learning outcomes the school is providing for students.

vi) Learn how various technologies are used today in the world of work, help students see the value of technology applications; and

vii) Participate in professional development activities to gain experience with various types of educational technology and learn how to integrate this technology into the curriculum.

Sell, Ray and Lovelace (1995) suggest that repeated viewing of the programme results in improved comprehension by 4-year old children. They attribute this effect to more complete processing of the formal features that enable children to focus on essential information critical to understanding the plot.

Tiffin and Rajasingham (1995) point that technological developments during the last few years have changed the education delivery system. Vast availability of computer networking has made the world a global village and its impact upon the teacher relationship is indeed tremendous. With rigid improvement of this communication networking, a new social pattern and a new approach to the education process has been created.

Deetya (1996) argued that ICT could contribute substantially to the improvement of schooling if it is appropriately used. The ICT by itself will not improve pedagogy. These can however, support and assist teachers who shift their pedagogies to make them more student-based, project-based and collaborative in nature.

Delores (1996) reported that there is no doubt that individuals' ability to access and process information is set to become the determining factor in their integration not only into the working environment but also into their social and cultural environment. ICTs do not have to prove the privilege of one culture over another. Educators almost universally use the book as a tool, adopting it to the needs of particular cultures. We also need to use ICTs universally in education, without adopting the economic and cultural assumptions that have driven to its rapid globalization.

Redid (1996) reported that sustenance use of teleconferencing can be justified only if it is backed by improvements in timing, access to telephone and fax facilities and high quality programme content, and adequate time for interaction. Information should be made available well in time to the learners about the teleconferencing schedule as well as related tele-materials. Therefore, it is desirable to attend to the details in the planning, designing, execution and evaluation of educational teleconferences

Means and Olson (1997) found that technology can support teachers' effort to engage students in long-term, complex projects by dramatically enhancing student motivation and self-esteem making obvious the need for longer blocks of time, creating a multiplicity of roles, leading to student specialization in different aspects of technology use, encouraging greater collaboration, and giving teachers additional impetus to take on a coaching or an advisory role.

Andersons and Collins (1998) concluded that the poor comprehension of both central and implied content should be attributed primarily to less developed knowledge bases rather than to any cognitive disability.

Kosakowski (1998) found that educators find impediments to evaluating the impact of technology. Such impediments include lack of measures to access higher order thinking skills, difficulty in separating technology from the entire instructional process, outdated technologies, need to develop new strategies for student assessment, ensure that all aspects of the instructional process –including technology, instructional design, content, teaching strategies, and classroom environment are conducive to student learning, and conduct ongoing evaluation studies to determine the effectiveness of learning with technology.

Phutela (1998) found that with regard to significant gains in the learning of concepts and practices, the teachers welcomed the technology but indicate the lack of opportunities to interact with the experts because of limited telephone lines. It demonstrates the potential of the technology in meeting the training requirement of larger groups.

Prakash and Lal (1998) conducted a study on presentation and production aspects in relation to the effectiveness of teleconferencing for orientation of primary schoolteachers. The findings of the study indicated that language presentation style, pace of presentation, clarity of graphs/charts/text used and teaching aids had a direct bearing on the effectiveness of teleconferencing. Design of the session should be learner-oriented and spontaneous to ensure active participation of learners, for which the experts/ presenters must be trained in teaching/learning through interactive technologies.

Subhayamma (1998) in his study on the impact of teleconferencing found that participants were apprehensive about certain aspects related to participating in question and answer sessions and also commented that inadequate time allotted for interaction negatively impacts the effectiveness of interaction sessions.

Trivedi (1998) found that interactive communication using satellite and long distance telephonic links contributed to the knowledge gain of the participants and conceptual understanding of the participants improved significantly

Tschanne-Moran (1998) described the affinity between teacher efficacy and (a) teachers willingness to implement innovation; (b) teachers stress level; (c) teachers willingness to stay in the field

UNESCO (1998) notes that the new technologies challenge traditional conceptions of both teaching and learning and, by reconfiguring how teachers and learners gain access to knowledge, have the potential to transform teaching and learning processes. ICTs provide an array of powerful tools that may help in transforming the present isolated, teacher-centered and text-bound classrooms into rich, student-focused, interactive knowledge environments. To meet these challenges, schools must embrace new technologies and appropriate new ICT tools for learning. They must also move toward the goal of transforming the traditional paradigm of learning.

Syer et. al (1999) in his study found that when new technologies are adopted, learning how to use the technology takes precedence over learning through the technology. The technology learning curve tends to eclipse content learning temporarily; both children and teacher seem to orient to technology until they become comfortable. Effective content integration takes times and new technologies may have glitches. It takes a few years until teachers can use technology effectively in core subject areas.

World Bank (1999) found that student achievement will be enhanced by positive teacher attitude but teachers generally lack subject mastery and confidence to teach and thus hinder the development of such attitudes. Teacher empowerment has direct significance to the learning achievement of students at primary level. The major identified weaknesses of the teaching force in primary schools of India are: poor subject matter, limited teaching skills, high absenteeism and lack of motivation.

Dept of Education, UK (2000) states that ICT can provide opportunities to engage and motivate children and meet their individual learning needs. It can make significant contribution to teaching and learning across all subjects and ages, inside and outside school, help link school and home by providing access to teaching and learning and to assessment and attendance data from home. It enables schools to share information and good practices, intelligent information management systems, integration between curriculum and management, monitor individual progress, use shared plans and other resources etc.

Kozma (2000) stated that technology motivates both students and teachers and energizes classrooms and makes a classroom a more interactive learning environment. In the world-link network learning and evaluation programme, one teacher in Peru said " I learned to break the routine of using the chalk and blackboard; world-link forced me to make my classes more interesting, more tangible; students are now more interested and effective.' The teacher and the researchers have said that world-link has helped students develop a sense of responsibility, the ability to work as team members, think creatively for solutions, and share knowledge

Perraton and Creed (2000) found that ICT is effective in raising teachers' capabilities in the classroom. ICT can also be used in various ways to meet the needs of deprived and marginalized children, those in remote areas as well as street children, refugees and war victims. It may very well be utilized for the physically challenged also like visually handicapped

Reil (2000) argues that much of what we now see as individual learning will change to become collaborative in nature. Reasoning and intellectual development is embedded in a familiar, social situation of everyday life; so social context of learning has a great deal of importance. Collaborative learning is, therefore, enjoying an increasing share in the curricula of schools, with ICT playing a central role.

Rosehella et. al (2000) identify four fundamental characteristics of how technology can enhance both what and how children learn in the classroom; i) active engagement, ii) participation in groups, iii) frequent interaction and feedback, iv) connections to real-world contexts. They also indicate that use of technology is more effective in teacher training, curriculum, student assessment, and a school's capacity for change

Jayatillike, B.G. (2001) conducted a study on evaluation of a study on teleconferencing in non-formal education and found that the viewers find the programme interesting and practically useful in their day-to-day activities. Viewers opined that the programme helped them to i) improve their knowledge (55%); ii) spend their leisure profitably (41%); and iii) find opportunity for self-employment (24%).

Jes and Co (2001) revealed that quality does not reside in the learning object itself, but in its pedagogical surroundings and in the teachers' capacity to easily link content with outcomes; with assessment data and with student profile information school can only be effective in enhancing learning and helping students achieve well-defined educational objectives when the standards, objectives, teaching, curriculum, resources, use of technology and assessment are all aligned. The content and method of assignment must be aligned to measure standards and objectives. Technology provides valuable tools to align the system to promote students learning by providing a means of monitoring alignment and communicating these initiatives to the public. Through the use of ICT, the teacher can alter and modify the presentation as per the need of the learners.

Lenhart et. al (2001) found that the gap is measured by the pedagogical practices associated with technology use in different schools. More than half (53 percent) of teachers in public schools who have computers use them or the Internet for instruction during class.

Murphy et. al (2001) stated that teachers use discrete educational software (DES) not only to supplement instruction, but also to introduce topics, provide means for self-study and offer opportunities to learn concepts otherwise inaccessible to students. The software also manifests two key assumptions about how computers can assist learning. First, the user's ability to interact with the software is narrowly defined in ways designed specifically to promote learning with the tools. Second, computers are viewed as a medium for learning, rather than as tools that could support further learning. There is a positive association between use of discrete educational software (DES) and student achievement in reading and mathematics, an association consistent with earlier reviews of the research literature on the effectiveness of computer-based instruction. Students in the early grade and in the middle school grade appear to benefit most from DES applications for reading instruction, as do students with special reading needs.

Thomas (2001) in his study said that because of easy accessibility, affordability and appropriateness for a wide range of teaching and learning situations a variety of audio medium such as audio cassettes, radio broadcasts, radio vision, radio text and interactive radio is being used in education.

Boster et. al (2002) examined the integration of student-based video clips into lessons developed by classroom teachers and found increased student achievement. More than 1400 elementary and middle school students in three Virginia school districts showed an average increase in learning for students exposed to the video clip application compared to students who receive traditional instruction alone.

Chandiram and Singh (2002) conducted a study on the use of teleconferencing as an input of the Distance Education Programme in eastern Orissa and revealed that anchorperson presented the session in a self-structured manner and panelists had good expertise in the content areas and were quite competent in answering the questions. Participants expressed their satisfaction over the language used by the panelists in delivering the content. At the same time it was found that participants gained maximum knowledge and appreciated the special strategies adopted for tribal areas in the context of girls education.

Marshall (2002) found strong evidence that educational technology "complements what a great teacher does naturally" extending their reach and broadening the students' experience beyond the classroom. There is an unprecedented need to understand the recipe for success, which involves the learner, the teacher, the content, and the environment in which technology is used.

Ringhstaff and Kelley (2002) stated that professional development is necessary to help teachers learn not only how to use new technology but also how to provide meaningful instruction and activities using technology in the classroom.

DEP (2003) indicates a positive impact of teleconferencing on presentation of contents, interaction between the experts and the learners, technology-related matters and activities conducted by the learners at the learning ends. Research studies have proved that if planned properly/systematically, teleconferencing can be an effective tool for teaching and learning at a distance

Dirr (2004) identified the following important evaluation strategies on the basis of his study i.e.,

i) Charge cross-disciplinary groups of teachers and technology coordinators with finding new ways that technology can help students to achieve goals of learning.

ii) Collaborate to create a technology plan for the school;

iii) Ensure that teachers are aware of the value of technology for all students, especially those considered at risk of educational failure.

iv) Provide extensive and research-based professional development opportunities and technical support to help teachers use technology to develop meaningful instructional strategies for students

v) Provide incentives, structures and time for teachers to participate in highly effective staff development to help them integrate technology into their teaching-learning.

vi) Find ways to make appropriate structural changes in the school day and class scheduling to support engaged learning with technology.

vii) Educate parents about new assessment methods that enable teachers and administrators to make judgments about the effectiveness of technology in supporting students learning, and.

viii) Use appropriate evaluation procedures and tools to determine the impact of technology use on students achievement based on the learning goals that were set. Consult evaluation sources such as Educators Guide to evaluate the use of technology in schools and classrooms, and share findings with the community.

DPEP, Orissa and DEP, IGNOU (2004) conducted a feedback study on radio broadcast programmes. The objective of the programme was to provide quality education to primary schoolchildren along with emphasis on attainment of minimum competencies in different subjects like mathematics, language and EVS. The sample of the study comprised of 600 children's, 600 teachers and 800 community members of eight different districts of Orissa. The findings of the study indicated that: about 65 percent of teachers, 67 percent of children and 58 percent of community members opined that the programme had average utility because of its appropriate selection of topic, adequacy of subject matter, correctness of content and organization of the programme. Further, in comparison to boys, girls reported that listening to the radio programme was somewhat problematic and suggested supply of radio to schools as a measure for the success of the programme. About 30 percent of total community members reported that the programme was highly useful, 58 percent felt it to be of average utility and only 62 percent among them were of the view that the programme had low utility. The participants attributed low utility to

- Broadcasting of programmes without much practical experience.
- Haphazard selection of topics,
- Inadequacy of subject matter.

- Limited duration of broadcast of the programme.
- Problem of electricity and dearth of radio sets in schools etc.

More than 53 percent of target population reported that story-telling method was more effective for learning of vocabulary and other topics in the language.

Gangappa and Chandraiah (2004) reports that TV, TV lessons and teleconferencing programme were more useful as compared to audio; television interactive programmes are likely to replace the face-to-face classroom teaching as the interconnectivity between the subject expert and the learner was live and interesting.

Agrawal (2005) reported that computer education has enormous scope for providing quality education training at all the levels. E learning has grown tremendously in less than two decades of Indian education.

Kay and Honey (2005) reported that ICT literacy reflects the need for students to develop learning skills that enable them to think critically, analyze information, communicate, collaborate and problem-solve, and the essential role that technology plays in realizing these learning skills in today's knowledge-based society. Representative of ICT literacy skills are the following six arenas critical to students' success in the workplace. i.e.

i) **Communicate effectively:** Students must have a range of skills to express themselves not only thorough paper and pencil, but also through audio, video, animation, design software as well as a host of new environments (e-mail, website, message boards, blogs, streaming media etc.)

ii) Manage and prioritize tasks: Students must be able to manage the multi-tasking, selection and prioritizing across technology applications that allow them to move fluidly among teams, assignments and communities of practice.

iii) Engage in problem solving: Students must have an understanding of how to apply what they know and can do to new situations.

iv) Ensure security and safety: Students must know and use strategies to acknowledge, identify, and negotiate 21st century risks.

Mishra, R. (2005) analyzed evaluative studies on audio research and reported that so far educational media has tended to focus more on the achievement of learners at the school level. This could be used for distance education for adult learners. With the expansion of FM radio in the country, the audio medium would make quality educational input accessible to a cross-section of society.

O'Dwyer, et.al (2005) found that while controlling both prior achievement and socio-economic status, fourth-grade students who reported greater frequency of technology use at school to edit papers were likely to have higher total English language arts test score and higher writing scores at fourth grade test scores on the Massachusetts Comprehensive Assessment System (MCAs) English/Language Arts Test.

Sudhish (2005) reported that the interactive radio group made greater gain in English language than the control group on both the comprehensive test and the speaking test with the gain on the comprehensive test being particularly striking in that the interactive radio group registered a two-fold gain compared to control group.

3.2 The Present Study in Relation to the above Literature

It is quite apparent from the findings of these studies that there is no consistency in the pattern of relationship between the use of technologies in the classroom and improvement in the performance of learners and other related variables. Overall performance of children, particularly in the Indian context, differs widely from school to school, block to block, and district to district. However, there is dearth of studies available, which have direct bearing on the present investigation. It is, therefore, in the fitness of tings that the present study aims at filling a research gap by way of study the effectiveness of EDUSAT Technology on the professional development of teachers working at elementary level.

Design of the Study

Research is best conceived as the process of arriving at dependable solutions to problems through planned and systematic collection, analysis and interpretation of data. It is the most important tool for advancing knowledge, for promoting progress and for enabling man to relate more effectively to his environment, to accomplish his purposes and to resolve his conflicts (Mouly, 1978). The value of research in education is that it enables educators to develop sound knowledge and strengthen the subject. The educational research ensures education a maturity and sense of progression.

Problems can be solved only on the basis of relevant data where a researcher sets up a research design capable of providing data necessary for finding the solution to his problems. However, the unit of research makes it impossible to say that one aspect is more crucial than another. The collection of relevant data is an important aspect in the conduct of research. Since obviously, "no solution can be more adequate than the data on which it is based." (Mooly 1964, p. 95)

The development of research approach and opinion survey was considered to be the most appropriate keeping in view the nature of the problem and the objectives of the study. Abdullah and Levine (1965) have stated, "The aim of the development research is to develop a new procedure, a programme or a product. For devising a new strategy, factual data are to be systematically gathered. On the basis of data collected, format and content is designed." "Methodological studies address the development, validation and evaluation of research tools or techniques" (Polit and Hungler, 1987).

The first and foremost requisite in any research is data without of which no study could be conducted. Hence, for collection of data, the researcher has to set up the design, i.e., to plan before hand, to explain the research, to describe the technique used for collection of the data for his investigation. He has to describe the sampling method, the population, the sample, the tools used, the method adopted and the procedure employed in the tabulation and organization of the data.

The researcher has to use sophisticated research methodology for arriving at a relevant point by which findings of the study can be used for the development of concrete strategy

In the previous chapter 'Review of Related Literature' pertaining to the present study, precise formulation of the research problem, rationale of the study etc, have been discussed. Keeping in view the above facts the researcher found it essential to describe the design of the study, which includes the followings:

i) Method of the study.
ii) Population of the study
iii) Sample of the study
iv) Sources of collections of data
v) Procedure of data collection
vi) Data treatment

4.1 Method of Study

The present study has been planned and implemented under Normative Survey Method. It aims at studying the effectiveness of EduSat technology on professional development of elementary schoolteachers. As such the purpose of the investigation was confined to a normative survey method and analytical approach.

If the scholar cannot clearly describe his method, the chances are that it is too vague and general to yield him satisfactory results (Hillway, 1956). So, there is the need to describe the method used in research work; the decision about the method depends upon the nature of the problems selected, the kind of data necessary, and its objectives. Keeping in view the above rationale the investigator has chosen the method for his study. i.e., so far as the research methodology is concerned, in the present study normative survey method has been used.

The term **normative** implies the determination of normal, typical conditions or practices. The term normative survey is generally used for the type of research that we intend to consider here, the research which purposes to ascertain what is normal or typical conditions or practices at the present time.

In the present study an attempt has been made to determine typical condition as regards the effectiveness of EduSat for professional development of teachers at elementary level of Sidhi district of the state of Madhya Pradesh.

4.2 Population of the Study

A population is generally refers to any collection of specified group of human beings or non-human entities like objects, institutions, units, areas, etc. Measuring the entire population though is not only impossible but also impracticable. So, it is essential to draw a sample from the population. The sample drawn from the population must be representative of whole population.

Since the elementary schoolteachers were the basic unit of this study, the universe consisted of eight blocks and schools of the Sidhi district of Madhya Pradesh. In the present study, sample teachers of elementary (primary and upper primary) schools were drawn from eight blocks of Sidhi district namely, Sidhi, Sihawal, Waidhan, Majholi, chitrongi, Rampur, Kusumi and Devsar

4.3 Sample of the Study

Multistage stratified random sampling technique was adopted for selection of various subjects of the study namely, blocks, schools and teachers.

At the first stage, blocks were identified. It was decided to cover all blocks of Sidhi district irrespective of rural and urban areas. As there are eight blocks, all the blocks were selected as the sample Block resource centre coordinator was selected as the sample of the study.

At the second stage, schools were selected from each block. Only three schools (i.e. one from block headquarters and two out of remaining two, one from rural and one from urban area of that block) were included in the sample.

At the third stage, teachers were selected from the sampled schools. The headmaster of the school and one teacher who had attended orientation programme for EduSat programme were selected as the sample of the study. If the headmaster happened to have undergone the orientation then an alternate teacher was selected on the recommendation of headmaster. The distribution of sample teachers of Sidhi district has been given separately in table 4.1.

Table 4.1: Distribution of Sample Teachers of Sidhi District of Madhya Pradesh

S.No.	*Blocks*	*Area*	*Teachers*		*BRCCs*
			Male	*Female*	
1.	Sidhi	Rural	02	04	01
		Urban	01	02	
2.	Sihawal	Rural	05	02	01
		Urban	01	01	
3.	Waidhan	Rural	05	01	01
		Urban	03	-	
4.	Majholi	Rural	06	01	01
		Urban	02	-	
5.	Chitrongi	Rural	02	04	01
		Urban	01	02	
6.	Rampur	Rural	07	01	01
		Urban	-	01	
7.	Kusumi	Rural	03	02	01
		Urban	02	-	
8.	Devsar	Rural	02	01	01
		Urban	03	03	

A look at **Table 4.1** shows that the number of subjects selected from each block in terms of gender location is broadly representative. Thus in all there are teachers from eight different blocks (i.e. rural teachers N=49, Urban teachers N=23; male teachers N=47 and female teachers N=25) and 8 blocks resource centers coordinators (i.e. one from each block). Besides, five teacher educators from Sidhi DIET have been included as the sample of the study.

4.4 Sources of Collection of Data

In order to achieve the objectives of the study, the following tools were employed for collection of data.

i) Questionnaire on various aspects of transmission through EduSat.

ii) Questionnaire on various aspects of professional efficiency of teacher.

iii) Interview schedule for block resource centre coordinators and teachers.

iv) Focus group discussion.

4.4.1 Overview of Questionnaire

Two different questionnaires were developed for the collection of quantitative and qualitative data.

One questionnaire covers the comprehensive aspects related to transmission through EduSat (appendix I). It was developed to assess the quality teaching-learning process transmitted through EduSat and other aspects related to it like technology-related issues, content of presentation, design and methodology of content development, language related issues etc. It has three parts. The first part of the questionnaire contains items related to transmission aspects of EduSat. The second part is related to teaching by the tele-teacher and the third part contains items related to perception of teachers on tele-teaching.

All items were presented in multiple-choice formats followed by subjective comments if any. No time limit was kept for the same to fill the questionnaire completely.

Another questionnaire covers five different aspects of professional competency of teachers, namely; i) communication skill; ii) curricular aspects and teaching-learning process; iii) planning and management of curricular aspects; iv) evaluation and monitoring aspects; and v) personal attributes related to professional development (Appendix II) aspect contains five items. The items are placed on a three-point scale. The purpose of the items was to assess the perception of respondents on various aspects related to professional competency; how far the Edusat programme contributes to the development of such variables as a means of professional efficiency in elementary schoolteachers.

4.4.2 Overview of Interview Schedule

An interview schedule was developed (Appendix III) for BRCCs/CRCCs and teachers of sample block. The purpose of the interview schedule was to discuss with the sampled teachers and BRCCs/CRCCs on various aspects related to the EduSat particularly issues related to administrative aspects and other related matters. An attempt was also made to include some items related to academic aspects of EduSat programme, transmission through EduSat, reactions of parents towards the EduSat as a whole. Through interview schedule, an attempt was made to study the perception of various stakeholders and collect some relevant suggestions for the improvement of transmission through EduSat.

4.4.3 Overview of Focus Group Discussion (FGD)

A Focus Group Discussion was organized at DIET Sidhi in the state of Madhya Pradesh. The purpose of the FGD was to collect some qualitative data, so that a clear picture of the effectiveness of EduSat on professional development of elementary schoolteachers' emerges. The members of the discussion included teacher educators, Block Resource Centre coordinators and teachers. In the first phase, discussions were organized in four different groups. Each group comprised of one teacher educator, two BRCCs and two teachers. A different topic was assigned to each group for discussion. -academic issues, administrative issues, monitoring of EduSat programme and teacher educators through EduSat etc. to Group I, II, III and IV respectively. Teacher educators in each group acted as facilitator and discussion was continued for one hour. In the second phase, discussion was held with all members together, where the researcher himself acted as a facilitator. The purpose was to elicit qualitative information on different aspects of EduSat programme particularly with reference to professional development of teachers.

4.5 Procedure for Collection of Data

As mentioned earlier, two new sets of questionnaire and one interview schedule were developed and employed for assessing the professional development of elementary schoolteachers and their perception towards EduSat technology. At the same time a focus group discussion was organized to collect relevant qualitative data to supplement the quantitative information obtained through questionnaire. For collection of data and from sample schools of different blocks of Sidhi district, necessary permission of the district project coordinators was sought. Block Resource Centre coordinators and heads of the selected schools were contacted in spot. The task of collection was accomplished with the help of two teacher educators from DIET, Sidhi. The teacher educators were given a short orientation as regards their activities and responsibilities during the time of data collection. The questionnaire was supplied to sample teachers through teacher educators personally. The purpose of the study was explained to them. General instructions with regard to responding to the items were thoroughly explained. Each sample respondent was requested to respond to all items sincerely. Respondents were assured that the responses would be kept strictly confidential.

Interview of BRCC and teachers were taken during field visit, with regard to the pre-designed interview schedule by the researcher and two teacher educators. Views, reactions, perceptions and suggestions were collected from sample respondents through face-to-face interaction.

4.6 Data Treatment

The data were analyzed to asses the current status of elementary teachers of Sidhi district of Madhya Pradesh on professional competency and their perception towards the EduSat technology through questionnaire, interview schedule and FGD. For the above purpose, the statistical technique of Chi-square test, and critical ratio were used. The qualitative data (through interview schedule and FGD) were systematically presented to reflect various aspects related to the contribution of EduSat on professional development of teachers and perception of various stakeholders on these aspects.

Necessary rapport was established through personal contacts. Or organizing Focus Group Discussion at DIET,

Sidhi a through discussion was made with the principal, DIET and other teacher educators, regarding the modus operandi of the FGD. Four teacher educators were requested to act as facilitator in four different groups during the FGD. Necessary information was given to facilitators regarding their roles and responsibilities during FGD and to make the discussion fruitful.

CHAPTER 5

Analysis and Interpretation of Data

In the present chapter an attempt has been made to analyze, interpret and present the results systematically. The focus of the study was to see the effectiveness of EduSat (Information Communication Technology) on professional development of elementary schoolteachers. The design and methodology adopted for the study have been discussed in the Chapter IV. To maintain the sequence and ease in presentation of results and formulation of important findings, the whole analysis has been divided into five sections. The first section (A) deals with the study of the effectiveness of information technology (teleconferencing) on professional development of teachers. The second section (B) is concerned with the study of the effectiveness of EduSat on academic achievement of children in primary grades. The third section (C) deals with the assessment of the quality of transmission of EduSat programme. The fourth Section (D) deals with the assessment of various aspects of professional development of teachers through EduSat programme. The final section (E) is concerned with analysis and interpretation of Focus Group Discussion held at DIET, Sidhi. Information presented in section 'A' and 'B' has been collected from the records of DEP-SSA. While information pertaining to section 'C' & 'D' is collected though a newly developed tool which is given in appendix. An exclusive F G D was organized at DIET. Sidhi for collection of qualitative data for the present study.

Table-5.1: Significance of Differences Technology-related Issues x SSA Functionaries

S.No.	*Item*	*Orissa*			*Rajasthan*			
		Agree	*Disagree*	*Un-decided*	*Agree*	*Disagree*	*Un-decided*	*C.R.*
1.	Technology of tele conferencing is easy to use.	84.8 N=123	11.7 N=17	3.5 N=5	95.5 N=277	2.8 N=8	1.7 N=5	3.37** 1.39 5.57**
2.	Technology motivated me to learn more and more	88.3 N=128	6.2 N=9	5.5 N=8	83.4 N=266	13.8 N=20	2.8 N=4	0.85 0.59 0.21
3.	Technology is easily accessible	97.9 N=142	2.1 N=3	0	82.5 N=261	14.5 N=21	31 N=9	4.04** 0.61
4.	Technology can be used for different types of teaching-learning.	80 N=116	6.9 N=10	13.1 N=19	84.5 N=242	8.3 N=24	7.2 N=21	1.01 1.14 0.63
5.	Visuals and sounds of teleconferencing were clear.	71.1 N=103	13.1 N=19	15.8 N=23	84.8 N=246	10.3 N=30	4.8 N=14	2.93** 0.21 0.48

S.No.	*Item*	*Orissa*			*Rajasthan*			
		Agree	*Disagree*	*Un-decided*	*Agree*	*Disagree*	*Un-decided*	*C.R.*
6.	Technology of tele conferencing provides scope for use of variety of visuals to support teaching-learning.	84.2 N=122	12.4 N=18	3.4 N=5	82.5 N=239	10.7 N=31	6.8 N=20	0.38 0.18 0.28
7.	Animation used in tele-conferencing stimulated any interest.	84.9 N=124	6.2 N=9	8.9 N=13	80.1 N=231	11 N=32	8.9 N=26	1.04 0.43 0
8.	I'm Interested in using the technology for enhancing my professional development.	91 N=132	1.4 N=2	7.6 N=11	83.8 N=843	7.9 N=23	8.3 N=24	1.8 9.34 0.07

(** significant at .01 level and * significant at .05 level)

5.1 SECTION A: Study of the Effectiveness of ICT Teleconferencing on Professional Development of Teachers

The first objective of the study was to study the effectiveness of Information Communication Technology (Teleconferencing) and the professional development of teachers. So, in this connection, the relevant date (research study) available at the office of DEP-SSA, IGNOU, New Delhi, have been taken as parameters. In the present context various aspects of teleconferencing has been studied and a comparative statement is made on the basis of perception of teachers from the state of Orissa and Rajasthan, which is given in Table-5.1.

Statistical analysis given in **Table 5.1** reveals that there are significant differences between the responses of SSA functionaries of Orissa and those of Rajasthan. SSA functionaries of Rajasthan and those of Orissa differ significantly and the differences are in favour of functionaries of Rajasthan. So far as technology of teleconferencing and its ease of use, clarity of visuals and sound, accessibility of technology are concerned, the SSA functionaries of Orissa have more favorable opinion than those of Rajasthan. The differences are significant at 0.05 level of significance. The differences on other aspects are statistically not significant

A perusal of Table 5.2 shows that the responses of SSA functionaries of Rajasthan and those of Orissa do not differ significantly from each other with regard to various aspects of content and its presentation in teleconferencing except the following: explanation of content made by the resource persons with illustration and examples and. logical and sequential organization of the content. While the inter-state differences for the former (CR=2.29) are significant at 0.05

Table-5.2: Significance of Differences Content and Presentation x SSA functionaries

S.No.	Item	Orissa			Rajasthan			C.R.
		Agree	*Disagree*	*Un-decided*	*Agree*	*Disagree*	*Un-decided*	
1.	Content was adequate and relevant to topic.	87.6 N=127	6.2 N=9	6.2 N=9	84.1 N=244	9.3 N=27	6.6 N=19	0.89 0.29 0
2.	Clear and simple language was used by the Resource Persons (panelists)	78.4 N=114	10.3 N=15	11.3 N=16	78.3 N=227	16.2 N=47	5.5 N=16	0.02 0.58 0.59
3.	Resource persons explained the content with illustrations and examples.	93.8 N=136	3.4 N=5	2.8 N=4	86.2 N=250	10.7 N=31	3.1 N=9	2.29* 0.51 0.03
4.	Content of teleconferencing was interesting.	86.2 N=125	11 N=16	2.8 N=4	83.4 N=242	12.8 N=37	3.8 N=11	0.7 0.18 0.09

S.No.	Item	Orissa			Rajasthan			C.R.
		Agree	*Disagree*	*Un-decided*	*Agree*	*Disagree*	*Un-decided*	
5.	Resource persons used a friendly style of presentation.	91.7 N=133	6.2 N=9	2.1 N=3	87.3 N=253	8.6 N=25	4.1 N=12	0.86 0.24 0.09
6.	Organization of content was logical and sequential	94.5 N=137	2.1 N=3	3.4 N=5	85.6 N=248	10.3 N=30	4.1 N=12	2.59** 0.48 0.07

(** significant at .01 level and * significant at .05 level)

level, those for the latter (CR=2.59) are significant at 0.01 level of significance.

Table 5.3 presents data in respect of significance of differences between opinions of SSA functionaries of Rajasthan and those of Orissa on programme design of teleconferencing. An examination of the Table 24 shows that there are significant differences between the two groups on four aspects viz., i) adequacy of the duration of sessions; ii) use of visuals by the resource persons to make the presentation interesting; iii) time for which visuals were shown and; iv) legibility of text and captions. The CRs on these aspects range between 2.59 and 3.62 and all of these are significant at 0.01 level. Differences between opinions expressed by SSA functionaries of Rajasthan and those of Orissa on other aspects of programme design are not significant.

An examination of Table 5.4 reveals that by and large there are no significant differences between the SSA functionaries of Orissa and those of Rajasthan. However there is one difference that is significant. SSA functionaries of Rajasthan feel that interaction with resource persons was adequate while those from Orissa feel that it was less than adequate. The CR on this difference is as high as 3.73 and it is significant at 0.01 level of significance.

Table 5.5 presents data in respect of significance of differences between the opinions of teachers of Rajasthan and those of Orissa on various items of the opinionnaire concerning impact of teleconferencing on teachers. It is obvious from Table 26 that except for two items (#3&5) the differences in opinions expressed by the two groups of teachers are significant. Teachers of Rajasthan expressed more favorable opinion on items 1, 2, 4, 10, 11, 12 and 13 and

Table-5.3: Significance of Differences Programme Design x SSA Functionaries

S.No.	Item	Orissa			Rajasthan			C.R.
		Agree	*Disagree*	*Un-decided*	*Agree*	*Disagree*	*Un-decided*	
1.	Duration of the session was adequate	57.9 N=84	36.6 N=53	5.5 N=8	78.4 N=227	10.3 N=30	11.3 N=33	3.62** 2.59 0.49
2.	The Resource person (panelists) used sufficient visuals to make the presentation interesting.	96.4 N=101	2.9 N=43	0.7 N=1	79 N=229	14.8 N=43	6.2 N=18	4.14** 1.95 0.23
3.	Division of session was judicious for presentation and discussion.	81.4 N=118	11 N=16	7.6 N=11	77.3 N=224	13.4 N=39	9.3 N=27	0.91 0.24 0.16
4.	Pace of presentation was appropriate	87.6 N=127	6.2 N=9	6.2 N=9	84.5 N=245	10.7 N=31	4.8 N=14	0.79 0.41 0.7

S.No.	*Item*	*Orissa*			*Rajasthan*			
		Agree	*Disagree*	*Un-decided*	*Agree*	*Disagree*	*Un-decided*	*C.R.*
5.	Visuals were shown for adequate time.	65.5 N=95	26.9 N=39	7.6 N=11	79.8 N=230	4.5 N=28	11 N=32	2.71** 1.97 0.32
6.	The text/captions were readable.	95.9 N=139	3.4 N=5	0.7 N=1	85.8 N=249	5.5 N=16	8.6 N=25	3.06** 0.2 0.28
7.	Sessions of teleconferencing were designed with appropriate teaching-learning inputs	91.8 N=128	6.2 N=9	2 N=8	848 N=246	6.6 N=19	8.6 N=25	0.78 0.04 0.4

(** significant at .01 level and * significant at .05 level).

Table-5.4: Significance of Differences –Inter-State Comparison Interaction x SSA functionaries

S.No.	*Item*	*Orissa*			*Rajasthan*			
		Agree	*Disagree*	*Un-decided*	*Agree*	*Disagree*	*Un-decided*	*C.R.*
1.	Time allotted for interaction was adequate	69 N=100	28.2 N=41	2.8 N=4	76.2 N=221	16.2 N=47	7.6 N=22	1.33 0.57 1.48
2.	Interaction with the resource person was adequate.	69 N=100	31 N=45	- -	88 N=255	4.1 N=12	7.9 N=23	3.73** 1.9 -
3.	Resource persons interacted effectively during the session.	83.4 N=121	15.2 N=22	1.4 N=2	80.7 N=234	10 N=29	9.3 N=27	0.63 0.56 0.38
4.	Responses of the resource persons were satisfactory.	82.1 N=119	8.3 N=12	9.6 N=14	83.4 N=242	7.6 N=22	8.9 N=26	0.29 0.07 0.07
5.	Sessions of teleconferencing motivated us to participate in interaction.	80.1 N=116	15.1 N=22	4.8 N=7	83.5 N=242	7.2 N=21	9.3 N=27	0.79 0.82 0.4

S.No.	Item	Orissa			Rajasthan			C.R.
		Agree	*Disagree*	*Un-decided*	*Agree*	*Disagree*	*Un-decided*	
6.	Participants interacted from different learning centre effectively.	92.5 N=131	4.1 N=6	3.4 N=5	81.7 N=237	8.3 N=24	10 N=29	1.12 0.33 0.48
7.	We clarified our doubts through telephone & fax.	92.5 N=135	2.7 N=4 N=146	4.8 N=7	83.1 N=241	9.3 N=27	7.6 N=22	2.56 0.44 0.46
8.	Questions of other participants from different learning centre promoted our understanding	95.1 N=136	2.8 N=5	2.1 N=4	89.4 N=254	5.5 N=21	5.1 N=15	1.93 0.22 0.23

(** significant at .01 level and * significant at .05 level).

Table-5.5: Significance of Differences Inter-state Comparison Impact on Teachers x Teachers of Orissa and Rajasthan

S.No.	Item	Orissa			Rajasthan			C.R.
		Agree	*Disagree*	*Un-decided*	*Agree*	*Disagree*	*Un-decided*	
1.	Teleconferencing helped me learn something new in the content area (s).	70.3 N=102	- -	29.7 N=43	84.8 N=246	4.48 N=13	10.72 N=31	3.11** - 1.95
2.	Teleconferencing helped me in organizing content of teaching-learning	64.1 N=98	- -	29.7 N=47	84.8 N=246	4.48 N=13	1072 N=31	3.72** 0.48 4.62**
3.	Teleconferencing motivated and helped me in developing TLM	30.3 N=44	3.4 N=5	67.5 N=47	37.9 N=110	0.7 N=19	38.6 N=161	0.85 0.16 1.34
4.	Teleconferencing helped me in handling problems effectively in classroom.	54.5 N=79	9.7 N=14	35.8 N=52	80.7 N=234	7.6 N=22	11.7 N=34	4.68** 0.22 2.48*
5.	Teleconferencing helped me in attending to individual differences in the classroom	47.6 N=69	17.9 N=26	34.5 N=50	37.2 N=108	8.6 N=25	45.8 N=157	1.37 0.98 1.41

S.No.	*Item*	*Orissa*			*Rajasthan*			*C.R.*
		Agree	*Disagree*	*Un-decided*	*Agree*	*Disagree*	*Un-decided*	
6.	Teleconferencing motivated me to undertake innovative teaching.	60 N=87	6.2 N=9	33.8 N=49	43.4 N=126	6.2 N=18	50.4 N=146	2.41* 0 2.05*
7.	Teleconferencing helped me understand the significance of inclusive education.	53.8 N=78	8.2 N=12	38 N=55	32.7 N=95	7.24 N=21	60.1 N=174	2.39* 0.1 2.05
8.	Teleconferencing helped me appreciate issues of girls' education	62.1 N=90	3.4 N=5	65.5 N=50	41.7 N=121	7.6 N=22	50.7 N=147	2.93* 0.34 1.82
9.	Teleconferencing helped me understand the importance of community mobilization.	61.4 N=89	2.8 N=4	35.8 N=52	37.2 N=108	5.2 N=15	57.6 N=167	3.40** 0.2 2.76**
10.	Teleconferencing helped me workout strategies for reducing dropouts	57.9 N=84	3.4 N=5	38.7 N=56	68.6 N=199	16.9 N=49	14.5 N=42	1.73 0.79 2.63**
11.	Teleconferencing helped me increase enrollment	58.6 N=85	3.4 N=5	38 N=55	69.6 N=202	16.2 N=47	14.2 N=41	1.8 1.76 2.57*

S.No.	Item	Orissa			Rajasthan			C.R.
		Agree	*Disagree*	*Un-decided*	*Agree*	*Disagree*	*Un-decided*	
12.	Teleconferencing helped me increase retention of children in classroom.	48.9 N=75	12.4 N=18	38.7 N=52	75.8 N=220	12.7 N=37	11.5 N=33	4.34 0.03 3.74**
13.	Teleconferencing equipped me to contribute better towards SSA goals	54.5 N=79	1.4 N=2	44.1 N=64	74.8 N=217	9.3 N=27	15.9 N=46	3.35** 0.38 3.12**

(** significant at .01 level and * significant at .05 level)

the CRs on these items range between 2.39 and 4.68. On the other hand, teachers from Orissa had more favorable opinion on items 6, 7 and 9. The CRs on these items range between 2.39 and 3.40. On items 3 and 5, the obtained differences were not significant. It is interesting to note that differences between opinions expressed by the two groups of teachers were significant at 0.01 level for items # 1, 2, 4, 9, 10, 12 and 13 while differences in respect of items #6, 7, 8 and 11 were significant at 0.05 level.

Table 5.6 presents the results of test of significance of the intrastate differences between the responses of BRC and CRC functionaries of Rajasthan and those of Orissa. The responses of BRC and CRC functionaries of Rajasthan are more favorable compared to those of their counterparts from Orissa except the responses on item No. 9 and all the differences are statistically significant at 0.01 level on all aspects of teleconferencing. BRC and CRC functionaries from Orissa as well as Rajasthan do not have significantly different opinions on item # 9.

5.2 Section B: Study of the Effectiveness of EduSat on Academic Achievement of Children in Primary Grade.

The second objective of the study was to assess the effectiveness of EduSat on academic achievement of children in primary grade. For this purpose, the official record (Research Study) available at the office of DEP-SSA, IGNOU, New Delhi, has been taken as parameters. The findings of the study are presented below systematically.

On examination of the Table 5.7, it is revealed that there is no significant difference between the Mean achievement (Hindi) of boys belonging to ROT and NON-ROT schools of Sidhi district.

Table 5.6: Significance of Differences Impact on Teachers (Perception of BRC and CRC Functionaries)

S.No.	Item	Orissa			Rajasthan			C.R.
		Agree	*Disagree*	*Un-decided*	*Agree*	*Disagree*	*Un-decided*	
1.	Improvement in Teaching-Learning methods used by teachers.	48.2 N=70	2.8 N=4	49 N=71	69.6 N=202	6.2 N=18	24.2 N=70	3.22** 0.27 3.32**
2.	Motivation in teachers to try out innovative teaching strategies.	46.9 N=68	2.8 N=4	50.3 N=73	61.7 N=179	12.7 N=37	25.6 N=74	2.10* 0.59 2.91**
3.	Modification in teaching behaviour of teachers.	40 N=58	5.5 N=8	54.5 N=79	61.6 N=179	127 N=37	25.6 N=74	2.88** 0.58 3.64**
4.	Change in perception of teachers for using technology for teaching-learning process.	42.8 N=62	5.5 N=8	51.7 N=75	61.3 N=178	12.7 N=37	26 N=75	2.54* 0.58 3.23**
5.	Difficulties experienced by teachers in participating in teleconferencing.	24.1 N=35	20 N=29	55.9 N=81	56 N=164	17.5 N=51	25.9 N=75	3.36** 0.11 3.80**

S.No.	Item	Orissa			Rajasthan			C.R.
		Agree	Disagree	Un-decided	Agree	Disagree	Un-decided	
6.	Preparation for the session at the learning end before teleconferencing.	22.8 N=33	28.3 N=41	51.1 N=71	57.2 N=166	14.8 N=43	28 N=81	3.61** 1.51 2.92**
7.	Fruitful Interaction between resource persons and participants.	42.1 N=61	7.6 N=11	50.3 N=73	63.8 N=185	11 N=32	25.2 N=73	2.98** 0.32 3.05**
8.	Facilitators facilitated interaction at the learning end.	34.5 N=50	13.1 N=19	52.4 N=76	55.5 N=161	121 N=35	32.4 N=94	2.59** 0.12 2.60**
9.	Teleconferencing is an effective medium for teacher training.	39.3 N=57	4.8 N=7	55.9 N=31	31.3 N=91	4.8 N=14	63.9 N=185	0.99 0 1.23

(** significant at .01 level and * significant at .05 level)

Table-5.7: Comparison of Mean Achievement of Children of STD V Belonging to ROT and Non ROT Schools of Sidhi District in Hindi

S.No.	*Category*	*Gender*	*ROT Schools*		*Non ROT Schools*		*Dif in*	*C.R.*
			Mean	*Mean %*	*Mean*	*Mean %*	*Mean %*	*Value*
1	Gen	Boys	11.35 N=30	45.42	12.56 N=15	50.24	4.82	0.32
		Girls	12.02 N=28	48.09	13.8 N=14	55.3	7.21	0.43
		Boys & Girls	11.69 N=58	46.74	13.18 N=29	52.72	5.98	0.53
2	SC	Boys	11.53 N=20	46.12	13.56 N=18	54.21	8.09	0.5
		Girls	8.23 N=15	32.92	17.27 N=09	69.08	36.16	1.58
		Boys & Girls	9.88 N=35	39.52	15.42 N=27	61.67	22.12	1.74

3	ST	Boys	13.44 N=13	53.75	11.23 N=10	44.9	8.85	0.42
		Girls	12.7 N=12	50.8	17 N=04	68	17.2	0.59
		Boys & Girls	13.07 N=25	52.28	14.12 N=14	56.46	4.18	0.15
4	OBC	Boys	11.54 N=07	46.15	14.94 N=16	59.76	13.61	0.98
		Girls	9.87 N=04	39.47	14.52 N=17	58.08	18.61	1.29
		Boys & Girls	10.71 N=11	42.82	14.73 N=33	58.92	16.1	1.63
5	All (Gen+SC+ ST +OBC)	Boys	11.97 N=136	47.86	13.07 N=53	52.29	4.43	0.55
		Girls	10.71 N=95	42.82	15.65 N=44	62.59	19.77	2.15*
		Boys & Girls	11.34 N=231	45.36	14.36 N=97	57.44	12.08	2.02*

(** significant at .01 level and * significant at .05 level).

Table-5.8: Comparison of Mean Achievement of Children of Standard V Belonging to ROT and NON-ROT Schools of Sidhi District in English

S.No.	*Category*	*Gender*	*ROT Schools*		*Non ROT Schools*		*Dif in*	*C.R.*
			Mean	*Mean %*	*Mean*	*Mean %*	*Mean %*	*Value*
1	Gen	Boys	9.12		12.56	N=15		0.88
			N=30	36.48	N=15	50.24	13.76	
		Girls	11.99		7.54			1.1
			N=28	47.98	N=14	30.16	17.82	
		Boys & Girls	10.56		10.05			0.17
			N=58	42.22	N=29	40.2	2.02	
2	SC	Boys	12.86		7.43			1.36
			N=20	51.44	N=18	29.73	21.71	
		Girls	8.64		8			0.13
			N=15	34.57	N=09	32	2.57	
		Boys & Girls	10.75		7.72			0.98
			N=35	43	N=27	30.86	12.14	

3	ST	Boys	8.63 N=13	35.33	10.43 N=10	41.73	6.4	0.13
		Girls	9.1 N=12	36.4	6.5 N=04	26	10.4	1.52
		Boys & Girls	8.72 N=25	34.86	8.46 N=14	33.86	1	0.06
4	OBC	Boys	10.75 N=73	42.98	10.55 N=16	42.2	0.78	0.05
		Girls	11.64 N=40	46.57	9.4 N=17	37.6	8.97	0.62
		Boys & Girls	11.19 N=113	44.78	9.97 N=33	N=33 39.9	4.88	0.5
5	All (Gen+SC+ ST +OBC)	Boys	10.39 N=136	N=136 41.56	10.24 N=53	40.97	0.59	0.07
		Girls	10.34 N=95	41.37	7.86 N=44	31.44	9.93	1.13
		Boys & Girls	10.37 N=231	N=231 41.46	9.05 N=97	36.2	5.26	0.89

Mean percentage of boys belonging to ROT school was 47.86 and NON-ROT school was 52.29 (C.R. = 0.55) whereas a significant difference is noticed with regard to Mean achievement of girls belonging to two types of school (C.R. = 2.15). It is surprising to note that this difference goes in favour of girls belonging to NON-ROT schools. Similar is the situation with regard to Mean achievement of whole (i.e. boys and girls together); for the whole the Mean percentage of children belonging to ROT school was 45.36 and for NON-ROT school was 57.44 with a C.R. 2.02. It is noticed that there is no significant difference between the students belonging to ROT and NON-ROT schools under different sub-groups like General (C.R. = 0.53), Scheduled Caste (C.R. = 1.74). Scheduled Tribes (C.R. = 0.15) and Other Backward Classes (C.R. = 1.63). But in all the above cases the Mean and Mean percentage of children belonging to NON-ROT schools are at the higher side than that of ROT schools. This poses a challenge to the effective utilization of EduSat network for the academic achievement of children.

On the perusal of Table 5.8 it is revealed that there is no significant difference between the Mean achievement of children in English at Std. V belonging to ROT and NON-ROT schools of Sidhi district of Madhya Pradesh. As a whole the Mean achievement of children (boys, girls, and boys+girls together) belonging to ROT schools are higher than that of NON-ROT schools. Though the differences are not statistically significant, yet it still reflects the efficacy of EDUSAT programme in academic achievement of children. Similar is the situation with regard to certain sub-groups like General Girls, General Boys and Girls, SC Boys, SC Girls, SC Boys + Girls, ST Girls, ST Boys + Girls, OBC Girls and OBC Boys + Girls.

Table-5.9: Comparison of Mean Achievement of Children of Standard V Belonging to ROT and NON-ROT Schools of Sidhi District in EVS.

S.No.	*Category*	*Gender*	*ROT Schools*		*Non ROT Schools*		*Dif in Mean %*	*C.R. Value*
			Mean	*Mean %*	*Mean*	*Mean %*		
1	Gen	Boys	13.02 N=30	52.08	13.5 N=15	53.6	1.52	0.09
		Girls	13.29 N=28	53.14	8.06 N=14	32.24	20.9	1.28
		Boys & Girls	13.16 N=58	52.62	10.78 N=29	43.12	9.42	0.83
2	SC	Boys	11.84 N=20	47.36	11.3 N=28	47.33	0.03	0
		Girls	9.92 N=15	39.67	16 N=09	64	24.33	1.15
		Boys & Girls	10.88 N=35	43.52	13.65 N=27	54.6	11.08	0.86

3	ST	Boys	11.47 N=13	45.87	14.05 N=10	56.2	10.33	0.49
		Girls	12.6 N=12	50.4	12.25 N=04	49	1.4	0.05
		Boys & Girls	12.04 N=25	48.14	13.15 N=14	N=14 52.6	4.46	0.27
4	OBC	Boys	14.59 N=73	58.39	14.25 N=16	57	1.39	0.1
		Girls	14.22 N=40	56.88	9.25 N=17	N=17 37	19.88	1.37
		Boys & Girls	14.41 N=113	57.62	11.75 N=33	47	10.6	1.08
5	All (Gen+SC+ ST +OBC)	Boys	12.73 N=136	50.92	13.28 N=53	53.1	2.18	0.27
		Girls	12.5 N=95	50.03	11.39 N=44	45.56	4.47	0.01
		Boys & Girls	12.62 N=231	50.46	12.34 N=97	N=97 49.34	1.12	0.19

On the basis of the above Table 5.9, it is revealed that the Mean percentage of Girls (M% = 50.03) and Boys + Girls (M% = 50.46) belonging to ROT schools is more than that of their corresponding counterparts belonging to NON-ROT schools in EVS of Std. V. But in case of Boys it goes in favour of children belonging to NON-ROT schools. In none of the cases the differences are statically significant. Similarly in different sub-groups, the Mean achievement of children belonging to ROT schools is at the higher side than their NON-ROT counterparts like General Girls (M% = 53.14), General Boys +Girls (M% = 52.62). ST Girls (M% = 50.4), OBC Boys (M% = 58.39), OBC Girls (M% = 56.88) and OBC Boys + Girls (M% = 57.62). This reflects that though EduSat programme is able to improve the achievement level of children, but much needs to be done with regard to impact of this technology for enhancing the level of achievement of children.

Table 5.10 gives the level of achievement of children belonging to ROT and NON-ROT schools of class V in mathematics. It was found that the Mean percentage of children in math belonging to ROT schools of Sidhi district is higher than that of their counterparts belonging to NON-ROT schools, though the differences are not significant but go in favour of children belonging to ROT schools. Similar is the situation with regard to certain subgroups as well like General Boys (M%= 54.96), General Boys + Girls (M%= 51.06), ST Boys (M%= 49.67), ST Girls (M%= 54.0), OBC Boys (M%= 47.29) and OBC Girls (M%= 49.39).

The above analysis shows that, though implementation of EduSat brings some changes in the perception of teachers and taught in the Sidhi district of Madhya Pradesh, yet a lot yet to be done to improve the effectiveness of this

Table-5.10: Comparison of Mean Achievement of Children of Standard V Belonging to ROT and NON-ROT Schools of Sidhi District in Mathematics

S.No.	*Category*	*Gender*	*ROT Schools*		*Non ROT Schools*		*Dif in*	*C.R.*
			Mean	*Mean %*	*Mean*	*Mean %*	*Mean %*	*Value*
1	Gen	Boys	11.79 N=30	47.19	12.86 N=15	51.44	4.25	0.27
	Girls	13.74	N=28	8.14 54.96	N=14	32.56	22.4	1.61
	Boys & Girls	12.76	N=58	10.5 51.06	N=29	42	9.06	0.01
2	SC	Boys	10.41 N=20	41.64	12.28 N=18	49.12	7.48	0.46
		Girls	10.21 N=15	40.82	10.96 N=09	43.84	3.02	0.15
		Boys & Girls	10.31 N=35	41.24	11.62 N=27	46.48	5.24	0.41

3	ST	Boys	17.42 N=13	49.67	8.83 N=10	35.3	14.37	0.69
		Girls	13.5 N=12	54	12.25 N=04	49	5	0.17
		Boys & Girls	12.96 N=25	51.84	10.54 N=14	42.46	9. 38	0.58
4	OBC	Boys	11.82 N=73	47.29	9.82 N=16	39.27	8.02	0.59
		Girls	12.35 N=40	49.39	9.1 N=17	36.73	12.66	0.87
		Boys & Girls	12 N=113	48.34	9.51 N=33	38.04	10.3	1.04
5	All (Gen+SC+ ST +OBC)	Boys	11.61 N=136	46.44	10.95 N=53	43.79	2.65	0.44
		Girls	12.45 N=95	49	10.11 N=44	40.45	9.45	0.93
		Boys & Girls	12.03 N=231	48.12	10.53 N=97	42.12	6	1.01

technology, so as to get a desired result in improving the achievement level of children. In none of the groups the difference is found to be significant.

It is revealed from Table 5.11 that the average achievement level of children belonging to ROT and NON-ROT schools of Sidhi district is at comparable level i.e. both categories of children are nearly at the same level i.e. in case of children belonging to ROT school M% = 46.36 whereas in case of NON-ROT schools, it was 46.78. It poses a great challenge to the effectiveness of technology and its quality as well.

In many cases the Mean percentage of certain subgroups belonging to ROT schools is higher than that of their counterparts belonging to NON-ROT schools, but those differences are not significant. This shows the mixed impact of EDUSAT technology on the academic achievement of children in various subjects. Again it was also noticed that in a few cases the Mean achievement of children belonging to NON-ROT schools is higher than that of their counterparts belonging to ROT schools like General Boys (M%=45.3 in ROT schools and 51.48 in Non ROT Schools). SC Girls (M%=37.0 in ROT schools; and 52.23 in NON-ROT schools), ST Girls (M%= 47.9 in ROT schools; and 48.0 in NON-ROT schools), and OBC Boys M%= 48.7 in ROT schools and 49.56 in NON-ROT schools). It is essential to make a thorough analysis of the programme of EDUSAT for deriving its maximum benefit to enhance the learning of children.

Table 5.12 shows the comparative profile of the achievement of children belonging to ROT and NON-ROT schools of Sidhi district of Madhya Pradesh in Hindi. It is clearly observed from the table that Mean percentage of

Table-5.11: Comparison of Mean Academic Achievement of Children of Standard V Belonging to ROT and NON-ROT Schools of Sidhi District

S.No.	*Category*	*Gender*	*ROT Schools*		*Non ROT Schools*		*Dif in Mean %*	*C.R. Value*
			Mean	*Mean %*	*Mean*	*Mean %*		
1	Gen	Boys	11.33 N=30	45.3	12.87 N=15	51.48	6.18	0.39
		Girls	12.76 N=28	51.04	9.38 N=14	37.54	13.5	0.84
		Boys & Girls	12.05 N=58	48.18	11.13 N=29	44.5	3.68	0.33
2	SC	Boys	11.66 N=20	46.64	11.14 N=18	44.57	2.07	0.13
		Girls	9.25 N=15	37	13.06 N=09	52.23	15.23	0.01
		Boys & Girls	10.46 N=35	41.86	12.1 N=27	48	6.14	0.48

3	ST	Boys	11.54 N=13	46.16	11.14 N=10	44.54	1.62	0.08
		Girls	11.97 N=12	47.9	12 N=04	48	0.1	0.01
		Boys & Girls	11.76 N=25	47.07	11.57 N=14	46.28	0.74	0.02
4	OBC	Boys	12.18 N=73	48.7	13.39 N=16	49.56	0.86	0.06
		Girls	12.02 N=40	48.08	10.56 N=17	42.27	5.81	0.64
		Boys & Girls	12.1 N=113	48.4	11.97 N=33	47.9	0.5	0.05
5	All (Gen+SC+ ST +OBC)	Boys	11.68 N=136	46.71	12.14 N=53	48.54	1.83	0.22
		Girls	11.5 N=95	46	11.25 N=44	45	1	0.1
		Boys & Girls	11.59 N=231	46.36	11.69 N=97	46.78	0.42	0.07

Table-5.12: Comparison of Mean Achievement of Children of Standard III Belonging to ROT and NON-ROT Schools of Sidhi District in Hindi

S.No.	Category	Gender	*ROT Schools*		*Non ROT Schools*		*Dif in Mean %*	*C.R. Value*
			Mean	*Mean %*	*Mean*	*Mean %*		
1	Gen	Boys	10.41 N=27	41.64	10.2 N=10	40.8	0.84	0.05
		Girls	8.64 N=40	34.57	12.32 N=18	N=18 49.27	14.7	1.06
		Boys & Girls	9.53 N=67	38.1	11.26 N=18	45.04	6.95	0.6
2	SC	Boys	8.67 N=20	34.65	10.56 N=14	42.24	7.75	0.45
		Girls	7.96 N=28	31.63	11.33 N=07	45.33	13.7	0.72
		Boys & Girls	8.32 N=48	33.26	10.95 N=21	43.78	10.52	0.84

3	ST	Boys	8.58 N=17	34.34	10.33 N=09	41.3	6.96	0.35
		Girls	7.68 N=14	30.74	8 N=17	32	1.26	0.09
		Boys & Girls	8.13 N=31	32.5	9.17 N=26	36.67	4.17	0.33
4	OBC	Boys	9.67 N=48	38.68	9.93 N=13	39.7	1.02	0.07
		Girls	9.43 N=36	37.71	8 N=16	32	5.71	0.39
		Boys & Girls	9.55 N=84	38.2	8.96 N=29	35.86	2.34	0.22
5	All (Gen+SC+ ST +OBC)	Boys	9.33 N=112	37.33	10.26 N=46	41.02	3.69	0.43
		Girls	8.43 N=118	33.71	9.91 N=58	39.65	5.94	0.77
		Boys & Girls	8.88 N=230	35.52	10.08 N=104	40.34	4.82	0.84

children (achievement in Hindi) belonging to NON-ROT schools is higher than that of their counterparts belonging to ROT schools in almost all groups and subgroups except General Boys (Mean percentage of children belonging to ROT school in 41.64% and NON-ROT school is 40.8%), OBC Girls (Mean percentage of children belonging to ROT school is 37.71% and NON-ROT school is 32.0%). In none of the cases the difference in Mean percentage is found to be significant as revealed from the critical ratio values.

From this observation, it is quite clear that children belonging to ROT schools are unable to compete with their counterparts belonging to NON-ROT schools. This really poses a great challenge to the huge investment against EduSat technology at elementary level. At the same time, it gives a sign to improve the transmission through EduSat, orient the grassroots level functionaries and develop adequate infrastructure for getting benefit of it to a large extent.

On examination of Table 5.13 it is found that there is no significant (statistically) difference between the Mean percentage of children in English belonging to ROT and NON-ROT schools of Sidhi district on the basis of critical ratio. The comparative profile presented in Table 42 gives a mixed result. In the above groups mean percentage of children is higher than that of their counterparts belonging to ROT schools. In al other cases though the difference is not significant yet the Mean achievement of achievers belonging to ROT schools is on the higher side than that of children belonging to NON-ROT schools. This shows the efficacy of EduSat technology with regard to the teaching-learning process at primary level.

On the basis of the comparison at children as a whole, it is found that the Mean achievement of boys in English

Table-5.13: Comparison of Mean Achievement of Children of Standard III Belonging to ROT and NON-ROT Schools of Sidhi District in English

S.No.	*Category*	*Gender*	*ROT Schools*		*Non ROT Schools*		*Dif in*	*C.R.*
			Mean	*Mean %*	*Mean*	*SD*	*Mean %*	*Value*
1	Gen	Boys	11.26 N=27	45.03	10.25 N=10	41.01	4.02	0.22
		Girls	10.45 N=40	41.82	10.03 N=18	40.13	1.69	0.12
		Boys & Girls	10.86 N=67	43.42	10.14 N=28	40.56	2.86	0.26
2	SC	Boys	10.38 N=20	41.52	10.76 N=14	43.04	1.52	0.09
		Girls	9.87 N=28	39.51	13.5 N=07	54	14.49	0.69
		Boys & Girls	10.13 N=48	40.5	12.13 N=21	N=21 48.52	8.02	0.62

3	ST	Boys	8.25 N=17	33	11.57 N=09	46.3	13.3	0.67
		Girls	7.07 N=14	28.27	9.74 N=17	38.96	10.69	0.62
		Boys & Girls	7.66 N=31	30.64	10.65 N=26	42.62	11.98	0.94
4	OBC	Boys	10.37 N=48	41.49	17.43 N=13	29.7	11.79	0.77
		Girls	9.72 N=36	38.86	8.38 N=16	33.5	5.36	0.37
		Boys & Girls	10.05 N=84	40.18	7.91 N=29	31.62	8.56	0.82
5	All (Gen+SC+ ST +OBC)	Boys	10.06 N=112	40.24	10 N=46	40	0.24	0.03
		Girls	9.28 N=118	37.11	10.41 N=58	41.65	4.54	0.58
		Boys & Girls	9.67 N=230	38.68	10.21 N=104	40.82	2.14	0.37

belonging to ROT schools is slightly more than that of children belonging to NON-ROT schools. But the situation is reversed with regard to achievement of Girls. Similar is the situation with regard to the achievement of Boys and Girls jointly. This indicates that EduSat system needs much more improvement.

Table 5.14 shows the comparative profile of the academic achievement of children in EVS belonging to two different types of schools (ROT schools and NON-ROT schools). It is revealed from the Table 5.14 that the4 Mean percentage of children belonging to ROT schools is on the higher side than that of their counterparts belonging to NON-ROT schools except in case of SC Girls, ST Boys and OBC Boys. No significant difference is found between the Mean percentages of children belonging to the two categories of schools. Though teaching through EduSat is able to improve the performance of children in the achievement of EVS, yet it is not up to the expectation as this level of achievement is slightly ahead of their counterparts. Systematization is the need of the hour to provide more benefit to children from EduSat technology.

Again on the basis of the comparison as a whole, it is found that the Mean percentage of children in EVS belonging to ROT schools is higher in case of Boys and Girls as well. Though the difference is not significant yet the value of critical ratio is on the higher side i.e. CR=1.5 in case of Girls and 1.82 in case of Boys and girls together. It is a remarkable achievement with regard to the contribution of EduSat technology.

Table 5.15 gives a comparative profile of the overall academic achievement of children of Sidhi district (belonging to ROT and NON-ROT schools). On the basis

Table-5.14: Comparison of Mean Achievement of Children of Standard III Belonging to ROT and NON-ROT Schools of Sidhi District in EVS

S.No.	*Category*	*Gender*	*ROT Schools*		*Non ROT Schools*		*Dif in Mean %*	*C.R. Value*
			Mean	*Mean %*	*Mean*	*SD*		
1	Gen	Boys	14.54 N=27	58.18	9 N=10	36	22.18	1.19
		Girls	12.78 N=40	51.12	7.6 N=18	30.4	20.72	1.46
		Boys & Girls	13.66 N=67	54.64	8.3 N=28	33.2	21.44	1.91
2	SC	Boys	12.61 N=20	50.45	12.5 N=14	50	0.45	0.03
		Girls	9.03 N=28	36.1	9.17 N=07	36.67	0.57	0.03
		Boys & Girls	10.82 N=48	43.28	10.84 N=21	43.34	0.06	0.01

3	ST	Boys	8.35 N=17	33.42	10.75 N=09	43.6	10.18	0.48
		Girls	9.47 N=14	37.86	5.4 N=17	21.73	16.13	1.29
		Boys & Girls	8.91 N=31	35.64	8.08 N=26	32.3	3.34	0.19
4	OBC	Boys	11.9 N=48	47.98	13.13 N=13	52.53	4.55	0.27
		Girls	10.83 N=36	43.31	6.8 N=16	27.2	16.11	1.1
		Boys & Girls	11.36 N=84	45.46	9.96 N=29	39.86	5.6	0.52
5	All (Gen+SC+ ST +OBC)	Boys	11.85 N-112	47.4	11.34 N=46	45.38	2.02	0.23
		Girls	10.53 N=118	42.11	7.24 N=58	28.97	13.14	1.51
		Boys & Girls	11.19 N=230	44.76	9.29 N=1o4	37.16	7.6	1.82

Table-5.15: Comparison of Mean Achievement of Children of Standard III belonging to ROT and NON-ROT Schools of Sidhi District in Mathematics

S.No.	Category	Gender	ROT Schools		Non ROT Schools		Dif in Mean %	C.R. Value
			Mean	Mean %	Mean	SD		
1	Gen	Boys	12.17 N=27	48.66	10.15 N=10	40.59	8.07	0.44
		Girls	10.36 N=40	41.42	7.09 N=18	28.35	13.07	0.95
		Boys & Girls	11.26 n=67	45.06	8.62 N=28	34.48	10.58	0.95
2	SC	Boys	10.93 N=20	43.71	11 N=14	44	0.29	0.02
		Girls	8.58 N=28	34.31	11.5 N=07	46	11.69	0.57
		Boys & Girls	9.76 N=48	39.02	11.25 N=21	45	5.98	0.45

3	ST	Boys	8.76 N=17	35.07	10.86 N=09	43.47	8.4	0.42
		Girls	8.25 N=14	32.99	7.36 N=17	29.44	3.55	0.18
		Boys & Girls	8.51 N=31	34.02	9.11 N=26	36.44	2.42	0.19
4	OBC	Boys	10.3 N=48	41.2	9.95 N=13	39.81	1.39	0.09
		Girls	9.89 N=36	39.53	7 N=16	28	11.53	0.8
		Boys & Girls	10.09 N=84	40.38	8.48 N=29	33.9	6.48	0.62
5	All (Gen+SC+ ST +OBC)	Boys	10.54 N=112	42.16	10.49 N=46	41.96	0.2	0.02
		Girls	9.27 N=118	37.08	8.24 N=58	32.95	4.13	0.54
		Boys & Girls	9.01 N=230	39.62	9.36 N=104	37.46	2.16	0.38

of comparison of subgroups, it is observed that in case of the Mean percentage of children of general group and OBC group, their academic achievement (Mean percentage) is higher for ROT schools. This holds equally good for subgroups like boys and girls as well. In case of SC and ST children, the situation is reversed. The difference goes in favour of children belonging to NON -ROT schools except ST Girls. So for two groups, it goes in favour of ROT schools (General and OBC) and for remaining two groups it goes in favour of NON-ROT schools (SC and ST).

Irrespective of groups, the overall comparison revealed that Mean percentage of children of Standard III of Sidhi district belong to ROT schools is higher (39.62%) than that of NON-ROT schools (37.46%). Similar is the situation with regard to the subgroup like Boys (Mean percentage of ROT schools 42.16% and NON-ROT 41.96%) and Girls (Mean percentage of ROT schools 37.08% and NON-ROT schools 32.95%). In none of the groups and subgroups, the difference in the Mean percentage is statistically significant.

A perusal of Table 5.16 indicates that the Mean percentage of children belonging to ROT and NON-ROT schools of Sidhi district in Mathematic goes in favour of children belonging to ROT schools in certain groups like General Boys, General Girls, SC Boys, ST Girls and OBC Girls etc. whereas in all other cases like SC Girls, ST Boys and OBC Boys, it goes in favour of children belonging to NON-ROT schools. This shows that the target of EduSat is achieved to certain extent, as the teaching through EduSat is yet to compete successfully for all subgroups. It is also indicated from the Table 45 that no difference is found to be statistically significant. It is a sort of challenge to the efficacy of teaching and learning through EduSat.

Table-5.16: Comparison of Mean Academic Achievement of Children of Standard III belonging to ROT and NON-ROT Schools of Sidhi District

S.No.	Category	Gender	ROT Schools		Non ROT Schools		Dif in Mean %	C.R. Value
			Mean	Mean %	Mean	SD		
1	Gen	Boys	12.45 N=27	49.79	11.14 N=10	44.56	5.23	0.28
		Girls	9.55 N=40	38.2	8.43 N=18	33.73	4.47	0.33
		Boys & Girls	11 N=67	44	9.79 N=28	39.14	4.86	0.43
2	SC	Boys	9.93 N=20	39.7	10.18 N=14	40.72	1.02	0.06
		Girls	9.45 N=28	37.81	12 N=07	48	10.19	0.49
		Boys & Girls	9.69 N=48	38.76	11.09 N=21	44.36	5.6	0.44

3	ST	Boys	9.89 N=17	39.58	11 N=09	44	4.42	0.22
		Girls	8.77 N=14	35.07	6.3 N=17	25.2	9.87	0.51
		Boys & Girls	9.28 N=31	37.14	8.65 N=26	34.6	2.54	0.21
4	OBC	Boys	9.26 N=48	37.06	9.32 N=13	37.3	0.24	0.12
		Girls	9.55 N=36	38.19	4.83 N=16	19.3	19.89	1.34
		Boys & Girls	9.41 N=84	37.62	7.08 N=29	28.3	9.32	0.92
5	All (Gen+SC+ ST +OBC)	Boys	10.38 N=112	41.53	10.47 N=46	N=46 41.9	0.37	0.04
		Girls	9.33 N=118	37.32	7.89 N=58	31.56	5.76	0.75
		Boys & Girls	9.37 N=230	37.48	9.18 N=104	36.72	0.76	0.13

On comparison of whole children irrespective of groups and subgroups, it is found that Mean percentage of children belonging to ROT school (37.48%) is slightly more than that of children belonging to NON-ROT schools (36.72%). Similar is the situation with regard to achievement of Boys (41.53% for ROT schools and 41.9% for NON-ROT schools). But achievement (Mean percentage) of Girls belonging to ROT school (37.32%) is higher than Girls children belonging to NON-ROT schools (31.56%)

5.3 Section C: Assessment of Quality of Transmission of EduSat Programme

The third objective of the study was to find out the perception of teachers and other functionaries on teaching and learning through EduSat. In this connection, a questionnaire was developed covering three important areas, namely; transmission related issues, performance of tele-teacher related matters; and tele-teaching related issues. An attempt was taken to collect perception of teachers through a three-point scale. The collected data are analyzed and interpreted as follows:

On examination of Table 5.17, it is revealed that with regard to receipt of prior information about the topic of transmission only 48.75 per cent teachers agreed whereas it was shocking to know that 28.75 per cent disagree with it and about more than 20 percent teachers did not respond on this aspect. Similar is the response with regard to relevance of the topic of transmission for professional development. In case of usefulness of the topic for the professional development of elementary schoolteachers, it is noticed that 58.75 percent of the teachers agreed whereas 15.00 percent disagreed and 26.23 percent did not respond to it. It was a

Table 5.17: Perception of teachers on Transmission Related Issues of EduSat Programme

S. No.	*Aspects*	*Responses (%)*			*Chi square Value*
		Agree	*Disagree Response*	*No*	
1.	Receive prior information about the topic of transmission	48.7 N=39	28.75 N=23	22.5 N=18	11.07 **
2.	Topic of transmission is useful for the professional development of elementary school teachers.	58.75 N=39	15 N=39	26.25 N=39	25.31**
3.	Topic is relevant for professional development	47.5 N=33	21.25 N=17	31.25 N=25	8.4*
4.	Duration of transmission on a topic is sufficient.	52.5 N=42	26.25 N=21	21.25 N=17	13.4
5.	Language used by the tele-teachers is simple and understandable	23.75 N=19	40 N=32	36.25 N=29	3.5

(** significant at .01 level and * significant at .05 level)

matter of regret that only 23.75 percent teachers agreed that language used by the tele-teachers is simple and understandable whereas 40.00 teachers disagreed on it and a large number of teachers (36.25 percent) did not respond to this item. This is a serious concern with regard to transmission of topic through EduSat technology.

There is a significant difference between the responses of teachers with regard to item no. 1, 2 and 3 i.e. the divergence is marked significant but the divergence with regard to item no. 4 and 5 are not significant.

It is clearly evident from Table 5.18 that only 15 percent of teachers of Sidhi district of Madhya Pradesh said that tele-teacher provide sufficient activities for teachers to perform in class whereas 55.0 percent of the teachers disagreed on it and 30.00 percent did not respond to it. The responses are similar with regard to performance of tele-teacher on developing interactive environment during presentation. It was observed that 33.75 percent teachers agreed that tele-teachers use varieties of activities for presenting the topic but 38.75 percent disagreed on the same and 27.3 percent did not respond. As far as the explanation of topic with suitable example and illustration is concerned, the responses are also similar (i.e. 36.25 percent agreed, 32.5 percent disagreed and 31.25 percent did not respond). 41.25 percent teachers viewed that tele-teachers seems to be prepared thoroughly for delivering the topic but 23.75 percent disagreed on it and 35.00 per cent did not respond to this item. The above explanations raise many questions with regard to performance of tele-teachers, which need to be considered seriously for improvement in future.

The difference in responses of teachers on item 1, 2 and 3 is not significant whereas it is significant with regard

Table-5.18: Perception of teachers on Performance of Tele-Teacher

S. No.	*Aspects*	*Responses (%)*			*Chi square*
		Agree	*Disagree Response*	*No*	
1.	Tele-teachers prepared thoroughly for delivering the topic	41.25 N=33	23.75 N=19	35 N=28	3.90*
2.	Tele-teachers use varieties of activities for presenting the topic	33.75 N=27	38.75 N=31	27.2 N=22	1.5
3.	Tele-teacher explained the topic with suitable examples and illustrations.	36.25 N=29	32.5 N=26	31.25 N=25	1.32**
4.	Tele-teachers provide sufficient activities for the teachers to perform.	15 N=12	55 N=44	30 N=24	19.56**
5.	Tele-teachers develop interactive environment during presentation.	22.5 N=18	57.5 N=46	20 N=16	20.9**

(** significant at .01 level and * significant at .05 level)

Table 5.19: Perception of Teachers on Teaching-Learning Process through EDUSAT

S. No.	*Aspects*	*Responses (%)*			*Chi square*
		Agree	*Disagree Response*	*No*	
1.	Faces difficulties from the presentation of tele-teachers.	22.5 N=18	57.5 N=46	20 N=16	20.9**
2.	Tele-teacher committed fundamental mistakes during presentation	38.75 N=31	26.25 N=21	35 N=28	1.98
3.	Standard of presentation is appropriate for elementary school teachers.	36.25 N=29	30 N=24	33.75 N=27	0.5
4.	Overall quality of presentation is satisfactory	41.25 N=33	33.75 N=27	25 N=20	3.18*
5.	Colleague's shows interest towards the programme of teachers training through EduSat.	27.5 N=22	41.25 N=33	31.25 N=25	2.42
6.	Teachers discuss about the topic after the transmission.	10 N=08	60 N=48	30 N=24	30.27**

(** significant at .01 level and * significant at .05 level)

to responses against item 4 and 5. That is the divergence in responses is marked significance only on item no. 4 and 5.

Statistical data presented in Table 5.19 reveals that 22.5 percent teachers said they face difficulties from the presentation of tele-teachers. But 57.5 percent disagree on it that is 57.5 percent teachers do not face any difficulties from the presentation of tele-teachers. The situation (responses of teachers) is similar with regard to perception of teachers on their colleagues (item no. 5). It is observed that 36.25 percent teachers are satisfied with the overall quality of presentation but 30.00 percent are not satisfied and 33.75 percent did not respond to it. It is clearly evident from the Table 5.3 that 60 percent teachers said that they do not discuss about the topic after the transmission. Only 10 percent teachers used to discuss whereas 30 percent teachers did not respond to it. This shows that there is no serious concern on the part of the teachers to watch the EduSat programme.

Difference in responses of teachers on various items on issues related to tele-teaching shows that there is a significant difference in responses to item no. 1 and 6 whereas in all other cases the divergence is not significant.

5.4 Section D: Assessment of Professional Development of Teachers through EduSat Programme

The fourth objective of the study was to find out the effectiveness o EduSat on the professional development of teachers. To get a clear picture of it, an attempt was made to develop a questionnaire and data were collected from teachers through a two-point scale. Five different aspects of professional development have been considered. The collected data is presented in the following order.

As revealed from the Table 5.20 about 67.5 per cent of teachers are in favour of the statement that transmission through EduSat focuses on making teaching-learning process more effective whereas 3.25 per cent do not agree on the proposition. Similar is the situation with regard to emphasis on effective organization of interactive session during T-L process. Surprisingly, 61.25 percent of teachers are not satisfied with the explanation of strategies of using TLMs for teaching effectively on the classroom. At the same time more than 52.00 percent of teachers disagreed on the tips to use ICTs for making T-L process realistic and interesting whereas only 46.25 per cent agreed on it. It was noticed that the teachers (57.5 per cent) are in favour of the aspect that the training through EduSat relates to work with other staff members, parents and community together but 42.5 percent of teachers says 'No' to it.

No significant difference between the responses of teachers was found with regard to: (i) explanation of strategies of using communication aids; (ii) providing tips to use ICTs; and (iii) training through EduSat relates to and work with colleagues, parents and community together whereas the divergence with regard to (i) focus on making T-L process more effective; and (ii) emphasis on effective organization of interactive session was significant.

From Table 5.21, we can conclude that more than 40.00 percent of teachers agreed on the aspect that EduSat transmission focuses on systematic organization of instructional objectives for classroom transaction and appropriate orientation of selection and use of T-L materials in classroom, but it was shocking to notice that 67.5 percent of teachers disagreed on the proposition that it provide

Table-5.20: Development of Communication Skills of Teachers

S.No.	*Aspects*	*Responses (%)*		*Chi-square*
		Yes	*No*	*Value*
1.	Focuses on making the teaching-learning process effective	67.5 N=54	32.5 N=26	9.8**
2.	Emphasizes on effective organization of interaction sessions during teaching-teaching processes.	60 N=48	40 N=32	4.2*
3.	Explain strategies of using communication aid (TLMs) for teaching effectively in the classroom.	38.75 N=31	61.25 N=49	4.05*
4.	Provide tips to use ICTs for making teaching-learning process realistic and interesting.	46.25 N=37	53.75 N=43	0.46
5.	Training through EduSat relates to and work with other staff members, parents and community together.	57.5 N=46	42.5 N=34	1.8

(** significant at .01 level and * significant at .05 level)

Table-5.21: Organization of Teaching Learning Process

S.No.	*Aspects*	*Responses (%)*		*Chi-square*
		Yes	*No*	*Value*
1.	Focus on organization of instructional objectives systematically for classroom transaction.	41.25 N=33	58.75 N=47	2.46
2.	Concentrate on sequencing the content and learning activities in a meaningful way.	51.25 N=41	48.75 N=39	0.05
3.	Orient in selection of teaching-learning material and use it appropriately in the classroom	45 N=36	55 N=44	0.8
4.	Provide opportunity of practice on presenting the content sequentially and appropriately.	32.5 N=26	67.5 N=54	9.80**
5.	Focus on development of suitable text items for evaluation and suggest remedy accordingly	22.5 N=18	77.5 N=62	24.20**

(** significant at .01 level and * significant at .05 level).

opportunity for practice on presenting the content sequentially and appropriately. Similarly, with regard to development of suitable text, items for evaluation and providing remedy, only 22.5 percent teachers agreed and remaining 77.5 percent disagreed on it.

With regard to concentration on sequencing the content and learning activities in a meaningful way, only 51.25 percent teachers agreed but 48.75 percent disagreed on the same. The divergence with regard to responses on item 4 and 5 was significant but on item 1, 2 and 3; it was not significant. From the analysis we conclude that responses of teachers (perception) on various items related to training through EduSat on organization of teaching learning process was just average.

It is revealed from the statistical figures presented in Table 5.22 that more than 50 percent of teachers are in favour of the proposition that EduSat transmission focuses on development of managerial skills like motivating students and potential of team work, using human resources appropriately and effectively for optimum development of children and provides opportunity to concentrate on developing technique of classroom management and plan it appropriately. It is encouraging to note that 67.5 percent of teachers expressed their satisfaction on EduSat transmission, which helped them to manage their time for curricular and co-curricular activities effectively, but only 48.75 per cent teachers said that EduSat technology develops their motivation on effective organizational capacity for professional development. From the above analysis, it was concluded that the EduSat in the form of information communication technology needs to be improved on various aspects so that it could attract the attention of all teachers working in the field of elementary education.

There is no significant difference between the responses of teachers on various aspects of management of curricular and co-curricular activities except with regard to effective management of time for curricular and co-curricular activities (Sl. No. 3) with Chi-square value 99.80**).

A perusal of Table 5.23 indicates that there is a significant difference between the responses of teachers with regard to various items related to evaluation and monitoring of curricular and co-curricular aspects except at item no. 4 where the divergence in responses is not significant. It was noticed that about 65.00 percent of teachers are of the opinion that they develop skill to use the concept of measurement and evaluation in and outside the classroom from EduSat transmission whereas 35.00 percent teachers do not agree on it. Only 12.5 percent teachers said that transmission of EduSat emphasizes on monitoring the progress of students and their own (teachers) performance.

Surprisingly, just 20-30 percent of teachers are in favour of the proposition that Edusat transmission i) focuses on how to measure behavioural outcome of learners, ii) provides adequate knowledge on construction of tools and techniques for assessment of learning outcome; and; iii) suggests measures to diagnose difficulties of children to provide remedial measure. It is a matter of serious concern that 70-80 percent of teachers are against the above aspects related to evaluation and monitoring.

It was noticed that from Table 5.24 that most of the teachers (72.5 percent) of Sidhi district hold a very favourable response on EduSat transmission focusing on academic as well as administrative aspects for professional development but at the same time 27.5 per cent of teachers did not agree

Table-5.22: Management of Curricular and Co-Curricular Activities

S.No.	*Aspects*	*Responses (%)*		*Chi-square*
		Yes	*No*	*Value*
1.	Focus on development of managerial skills like motivating students and potential of team work.	57.5 N=46	42.5 N=34	1.8
2.	Develop motivation on effective organizational capacity for professional development.	48.75 N=39	51.25 N=41	0.05
3.	Stress on effective management of time for curricular and co-curricular activities.	67.5 N=54	32.5 N=26	9.80**
4.	Focus on using human resources appropriately and effectively for optimum development of children	53.75 N=43	46.25 N=37	0.45
5.	Provide an opportunity to concentrate on developing technique of classroom management and plan it appropriately.	56.25 N=45	43.75 N=35	1.89

(** significant at .01 level and * significant at .05 level)

Table-5.23: Evaluation and Monitoring of Curricular and Co-curricular Aspects

S.No.	*Aspects*	*Responses (%)*		*Chi-square*
		Yes	*No*	*Value*
1.	Skillful use of the concept of measurement of evaluation in and out side the classroom.	65 N=52	35 N=28	7.20**
2.	Focus on how to measure behavioral outcome of learners in and around the classroom	26.25 N=21	73.75 N=59	18.04**
3.	Provide adequate knowledge on construction of tools and techniques for the assessment of the learning outcomes.	28.75 N=23	71.25 N=57	14.44**
4.	Emphasizes on monitoring the progress of the students as well as their own performance	42.5 N=34	57.5 N=46	1.8
5.	Suggest measures to diagnose difficulties of children to provide remedial action.	20 N=16	80 N=64	58.8**

(** significant at .01 level and * significant at .05 level)

Table-5.24: Personal Attribute as a Means of Professional Development

S.No.	*Aspects*	*Responses (%)*		*Chi-square Value*
		Yes	*No*	
1.	Provide maximum opportunity for developing the interest and curiosity of teachers in using ICTs for classroom teaching-learning process.	36.25 N=29	63.75 N=51	6.05*
2.	Scope for all round development of children and teaching profession by the effective use of technology	46.25 N=37	53.75 N=43	0.45
3.	Focuses on academic as well as administrative aspects for professional efficiency.	72.5 N=58	27.5 N=22	16.20**
4.	Develop interest to focus more on instructional objectives and its outcome.	52.5 N=42	47.5 N=38	0.2
5.	Bring a change in overall personality and perception of teacher as a professional	28.75 N=23	71.25 N=57	8.45**

(** significant at .01 level and * significant at .05 level)

on it. It was also noticed that 45-55 percent of teachers agreed that EduSat transmission provides (i) scope for all round development of children and teaching profession by effective use of technology; (ii) and develops interest to focus more on instructional objectives and its outcome.

Again data in Table 5.24 reflects the poor responses of teachers with regard to potentials of EduSat to bring a change in overall personality and perception of teachers as a professional (28.75 percent) and providing opportunity for developing the interest and curiosity of teachers in using ICTs for classroom T-L process (36.25 per cent). The divergence of response as obtained from teachers is significant at Sl No.1 (chi-square value 6.05*), Sl. No.3 (chi-square value is 16.2**) and Sl No. 5 (Chi-square value = 8.45**) whereas it was found to be not significant with regard to (i) scope or all round development of children and teaching profession by effective use of technology; and (ii) develop interest to focus more on instructional objectives and its outcome.

5.5 Section E: Assessment of the Perception of Teachers on Various Aspects of EduSat through Focus Group Discussion

The fifth object of the present study was to study the perception of teachers towards teaching and learning through EduSat programme. To achieve this objective, a Focus Group Discussion has been organized at DIET, Sidhi where five teacher educators and 8 BRCCs and 16 teachers have participated. An attempt was made to have a fruitful discussion with them about overall aspects of EduSat programme in different phases. The findings of the discussion are presented below though different headings.

5.6 Focus Group Discussion (FGD)

The researcher organized a Focus Group Discussion (FGD) in the state of Madhya Pradesh at DIET Sidhi. The purpose of the discussion was to collect some qualitative relevant information, so that a clear picture of the effectiveness of EduSat on professional development of SSA functionaries emerges. The members of the discussion included teacher educators, block resource centre coordinators and teachers. Discussions were organized in different groups. During the first phase, one teacher educator of each group acted as head with all members together, where the researcher himself acted as a facilitator.

5.6.1 Phase I: Group – I (Academic Issues Related to EduSat)

- Focus of transmission is on subject, content and class for which it is meant; presentation of content should not deviate from normal transactional strategy. It must correspond to level of children and academic calendar as well. More emphasis is given on difficult and problematic issues related to content and its presentation.
- Teachers at learning are instructed to carry our pre and post-transmission discussion with children for comprehensive clarity on the content.
- The difficult topic and concepts of a particular subject may be repeated again and again to clear the understanding of children. At the same time pedagogical part may also be highlighted for the benefit of teacher.
- New methods with adequate innovation are

implemented in delivering the lesson so as to make it interesting and effective. Teachers of all elementary level should be given training as to how to facilitate teaching-learning process during transmission. Active involvement of teachers plays a major role in developing interest and curiosity of learners.

- Challenging activity may be given to children as homework but unfortunately this aspect is missing from EduSat transmission.
- Mostly lecture method is being adopted by tele-teachers for presentation of content. Hardly demonstration and discussion method is used. It deteriorates the level of presentation and understanding of children.
- Tele-teachers do not focus on local dialect, which creates problem in understanding as the target group is from typical rural background.
- Care is laid on the pace of presentation, which is essential for effective teaching-learning process.
- Language presentation is simple and clear to alter the attention of all target groups.

GROUP II
(Administrative Issues Related to EduSat)

- Provision should be made by authorities to orient one/two persons from local community for maintenance of ROTs and accountability be fixed on them so that teachers, BRC/CRC functionaries can spare more time for academic activities.
- District administrators should make a random check/supervision at least once in a month, so as to make the

block authority alert and boost the morality of teachers.

- Adequate number of teachers should be appointed at each school so that normal teaching-learning process can be carried out efficiently as per prescribed timetable.
- Staff of each school must discuss together to find out ways and means of solving various minute problems related to ROT or EduSat transmission or adjusting school timetable etc.
- Teachers working at primary and elementary school should be free from non-academic activities, so that they can use their time for academic improvement of children and be able to plan constructively for overall development of teaching-learning processes with the help of EduSat transmission.
- Record of each and every telecast programme should be maintained properly at learning end to provide feedback for improvement in future.

Group III (Monitoring Issues Related to EduSat)

- No ROT is installed at BRC and CRC level, but presence of which is an essential requirement for effective monitoring.
- Provision be made from district authority to supervise the programme monthly and submit the report to state level authorities, but no adequate steps have been taken up so far.
- HM of elementary school where adequate staff is available, be given responsibility to send their teachers for monitoring nearby schools.

- Detailed programme schedule indicating class, subject and topic be circulated well in advance to all schools for information and necessary action.
- At each block, a monitoring team should be constituted for supervising, visiting schools during transmission period and they need to be empowered to send confidential report directly to state authorities.
- Record of EduSat programme related to transmission should be maintained regularly at school as well as at block level.
- Each BRC must send a supervisory report of at least one school in a day. It should be made compulsory.
- Purpose of monitoring must be constructive and suggestive rather than faultfinding.
- VEC may be given authority to monitor the programme of EduSat so that regularity can be expected to certain level.

5.6.2 Phase II: Overall Focus Group Discussion

- DIET functionaries are not involved in monitoring, supervision and assessment of EduSat transmission in Sidhi district, which is an unfortunate situation with regard to improvement of EduSat programme.
- More emphasis must be given on sequential development of content and its systematic presentation according to level of children.
- Variety of activities should be incorporated in presenting the difficult content and scope for revision and recapitulation must be kept open for children.
- A separate room with adequate seating arrangements

needs to be developed at each school so that regular teaching learning processes of other classes will not be disturbed.

- Pre and post-transmission activity is important for enhancing academic performance of children; so at every school a separate teacher may be appointed to look into the EduSat activities, its feedback and to plan for its remedial activity etc.
- BRCCs hardly supervises the school during transmission
- Tele-teacher simply uses lecture method in many cases for presentation of topic; they hardly follow demonstration and other innovation and sometimes commit mistakes in presentation particularly in teaching mathematics and science topics
- Hardly teachers of elementary school observe the programme transmitted on Saturday.
- Many teachers said that it is like normal classroom teaching; we do not find any interaction and innovative techniques related to pedagogy.
- State and district administration hardly take any measures for inspection, supervision, monitoring for improving the quality of EduSat programme.
- Most of the ROTs are not in functional condition but higher authorities remain silent about it; from a few schools the ROT and TV sets have been stolen but no action has been initiated so far.
- Language used by tele-teachers during presentation is a hurdle for the students as the schools are in a rural belt and they prefer local dialect rather than common language.

5.7 Strength of EduSat Programme as Suggested by the Teachers from Sidhi District during FGD

- Sometimes EDUSAT transmission covers new innovative topics, methods and strategies with regard to the need and demand of teacher's professional growth. It provides platform to enhance the participant's knowledge and understanding.
- It helps develop capacity building of teachers, BRCCs/ CRCCs and other functionaries of SSA, for quality elementary education.
- It is quite helpful in disseminating messages/ information to grassroots levels and reaching a large target group uniformly.
- It provides contextual and conceptual clarification of teachers within a short time with the help of quality resource person.
- It provides solutions to the problem and acquaints all individuals with the varieties of problems and remedy as well.
- It develops teacher confidence by enhancing their knowledge of knowledge of content and transactional strategies.
- The programme of transmission through EduSat is very effective with regard to use of TLMs and transactional strategies.
- It provides a variety of activities and strategies for its implementation.
- Programmes of EduSat improve professional competencies of teachers and upgrade their knowledge.

- EduSat programmes motivate teachers, teacher educators and other functionaries of SSA to develop and use teaching-aids and develop new TLMs for classroom transaction.
- It reaches at large target group on a number of issues, unites all teachers together and provides a valuable platform for discussion.
- EduSat transmission promotes the use of new techniques in the teaching-learning process.

5.8 Limitation of EDUSAT Programmes as Suggested by Teachers of Sidhi District during FGD

- Only a particular group of teachers (schools where ROT is installed) gets the opportunity to regularly participate in the programme.
- Most of the teachers do not show adequate interest in attending the programme. They are of the view that there is nothing innovative; so we do not find anything new to learn.
- There is no interaction between teaching and learning end. So we could not clarify our doubts and solve our problems.
- It creates a difference with regard to teaching and learning as well as school atmosphere, as there is no ROT in each and every school (only available at selected schools).
- There is no monitoring system at the district and the block level on the process of EduSat transmission and its outcome.
- There is no prior communication about field level

functionaries with regard to subject, topic and class for which transmission is available.

- No pre and post-transmission preparation at the learning end.
- Programmes are not related to the basic problems of teachers in their classroom and at the workplace.
- Learning environment is not properly maintained in terms of water, seating arrangement etc. There are always problems related to infrastructure.

5.9 Perception of Headmasters on EDUSAT Programme

- Programme of EduSat is quite helpful to students and teacher but the programme, which is transmitted is not so interesting. It could have improved in many aspects.
- Teaching through EduSat is found to be just like normal classroom teaching. There is no improvement with regard to use of technology for making it more interesting.
- There is a change in perception of students, teachers and parents as well with regard to teaching learning through Television.
- Not only students, teachers are also benefited to a great extent through EduSat transmission. It helps in providing clarity with regard to teaching strategies; particularly it helps the teachers to develop English pronunciation skill.

5.10 Suggestions of Teachers for Improvement of EDUSAT Programme

- All teachers and active members of VEC are given

basic training in maintenance of ROT and other fundamental aspects related to it rather than only teachers from a school.

- Adjustment of time is essential to provide enough scope for discussion, debate and interaction with children before and after transmission.
- There is no continuity in topic, which is transmitted. It creates a lot of confusion in children. Care needs to be taken to avoid such difficulties so that participation of children with adequate interest can be ensured.
- There is no clear instruction and guidelines for teachers about their roles and responsibilities during transmission. Even no handbook or study material is provided to teachers for understanding. For making the programme more effective, it is essential to develop a handbook for teachers indicating do's and don't on various aspects.
- Any problem related to signal is dealt immediately, so that transmission takes place without hindrance.
- Quality of programme is improved time to time and local teachers from rural areas should be given an opportunity to present lesson from studio, to encourage them and develop their potentiality on effective teaching.

5.11 Suggestions of BRC/CRC Functionaries for Improvement of EDUSAT Programme

- A topic, which is difficult, should be considered for broadcasting. A teacher faces a lot of difficulties with regard to adjusting the normal school timetable. So steps should be taken to synchronize school timetable and transmission of timetable.

- H.M. /one teacher from each school should be given recurrent training so that he/she is able to handle problems related to ROTs. In many schools ROTs are not in functional condition; so it creates a lot of problem to children and teachers as well.
- Provision is made to allocate a definite budget for monitoring and supervision of EDUSAT programme.
- Problems related to functioning of ROT should be resolved on priority basis.
- Schedule of transmission must be supplied to BRC and CRC in advance so that necessary steps can be taken to support school functionaries and monitoring strategies can be developed accordingly.
- Monitoring aspect is decentralized and responsibility and accountability need to be fixed to make it more and more effective.
- Presentation aspect needs to be improved to facilitate the interest of learners and teachers.
- Schools where ROT is installed must be equipped with adequate teachers so that corrective measures can be taken to make the programme of EDUSAT easily and effectively available to children.
- BRC/CRC functionaries and teachers of primary and elementary schools should be more involved in academic matters than other administrative aspects.

5.12 Suggestions of Teacher Educators for Improvement of EDUSAT Programme

- Transmission of EDUSAT programme may include games and activities at primary level. It is essentially meant to boost up the interest and moral strength of children. At the same time retention of children at schools could be intensified as well.

- Duration of transmission on each topic may be increased to enable the children to understand the content more precisely and definitely. Because of short time period, children face difficulty in recapitulating the content matter.
- There is a lot of problem with regard to operational aspect of ROTs. Care must be taken so that each and every ROT set operates as per schedule and time.
- Effective monitoring is essential for effective learning.
- Accountability should be entrusted to DIET functionaries for making the monitoring aspect more sound and effective.
- Only a different topic of each subject should be considered for broadcasting. The level of difficulty should be considered from teacher's perspectives so that it can attract the attention and interest of teachers to know about the pedagogical aspects for delivering the content.
- For each programme, the school HM needs to appoint one teacher as programme in-charge preferably the subject teachers. The programme in-charge should initiate discussion with the children after transmission and assign adequate assignment to children for homework.
- Topics related to moral education may be included for transmission, which will serve as guidance for the elementary schoolchildren.
- Instead of covering all subjects, priority may be given to one/two subjects preferably English and mathematics

so that more and more lessons can be covered through EDUSAT programme.

- Provision may be made to analyze the performance of children, immediately after the programme, so that necessary feedback can also be collected about the programme, on the basis of which remedial steps can be taken up.

5.13 Perception of Teachers on EduSat Programme

- Though the programme of EduSat is quite useful yet because of the unavailability of adequate number of teachers in schools, the programme is not being able to attract the attention and interest of children.
- We do not find interest in children to watch the programme telecast. Sometimes children are of the opinion that classroom teaching is quite good than teaching through EduSat.
- During classroom teaching, we teach considering the basic need and requirement of children but teaching through EduSat does not consider the same; rather it is stereotype activity.
- In certain cases the presentation made by tele-teacher is quite interesting where children attended such programme attentively,
- Some teachers are of the opinion that the programme of EduSat helps them a lot to improve their academic activity while there are teachers who said that the teaching needs improvement for attracting attention of teachers.

5.14 Perception of Students on EduSat Programme

- The programme of EduSat is not as good as classroom teaching.
- The duration for which captions and diagrams etc are shown needs be increased, so that we can write the relevant matter from the screen.
- Tele-teachers don't to repeat the important aspects during teaching, which creates difficulty in understanding the whole lesson.
- Programme of Hindi, and English are found to be interesting than other subjects.
- A teacher interacts with students during and after the programme as per the requirement, which clarifies our doubts. The voice of tele-teacher is not clear; it creates problems in understanding the topic.
- Students are excited about the programme of EduSat. They show interest to watch the programmes of EduSat regularly. Their perception is quite positive with regard to attending the school and watching television.

5.15 Perception of Parents on EduSat Programme

- Parents are of the opinion that interest of children is being increased day by day to attend the school for watching television.
- The programme of EduSat was found to be useful for children providing exposure to them.
- Teachers are not able to give enough attention on EduSat programme, as there are only one or two teachers in school.

- Very few parents said that their children discuss with them the transmission through EduSat and other matters related to EduSat programme.
- No parents are invited to school to watch the programme of EduSat. Even parents never come to school to know about the performance of their children.

Summary and Conclusion

6.1 Context of the Study

Sidhi is an educationally backward district in comparison to other districts such as Indore and Bhopal in the state of Madhya Pradesh. It is dominated by rural area/population. Sidhi district comprises of 8 Blocks, 149 cluster resource centers and 1753 villages. Overall literacy in the district is 52.80 percent, which is much lower than the literacy level of Indore and Bhopal districts. In Indore the literacy rate was 74.80 percent and in Bhopal it was 75.10 percent. The female literacy in Sidhi district i.e. 36.40 per cent is also very low in comparison to all these districts. To provide easy access to all children of 6-14 years age group in this district, there are 1455 Education Guarantee Scheme/Alternative Schooling Centers. In 2003, there were 22.80 per cent single teacher primary schools in the district, which is also very high in the Sidhi district in comparison to Indore (10.30 percent) and Bhopal (13.00 per cent) districts. There is less number of urban schools in Sidhi. Majority of the schools in the district are being financed and managed by the State government. There are 3187 primary and 988 upper primary schools in the district of Sidhi with enrolment of approximately 141.78 lakh children (76.48 lakh boys and 65.30 lakh girls) enrolled in class I to VIII in the state. There are still 4.28 lakh children in the age group of 6-14 years who are out of school. The actual achievement in terms of retention in schools up to class VIII is still problematic in the state. The dropout rate at primary and elementary school level in M.P. is 21.4 and 21.5 per cent respectively. For classes beyond VIII and up to XII, the aspect of dropout is even more problematic Similar is the situation in some other neighboring Hindi speaking states. The major factor for such an abnormal dropout rate seems to be the poor quality of education and a very weak and inadequate system of teacher education. The later results in adversely affecting the capabilities of elementary schoolteachers and hence the quality of learning at elementary school.

6.1.1 Objectives of the EDUSAT Pilot Project

EDUSAT networks with extensive reach and connectivity can effectively empower teachers and improve quality of elementary education in the majority of schools in district of Sidhi and a few other schools in adjoining districts of other states. The objectives of this project were to: i) ensure availability of quality content online and through a variety of access devices in schools; ii) enrich existing curriculum and pedagogy at different levels by employing all the technologies available, through the EDUSAT including virtual classrooms, video on demand etc.; iii) promote a shift from current passive learning based on instructors to active learning; iv) support to total literacy/adult education and compulsory education for all in the age group of 6-14 years; v) in-service and recurrent training of schoolteachers, continuous up-gradation of their knowledge and skills; vi)create an enabling environment for the optimal use of the EduSat in providing teacher training; vii) training of teachers and master trainers in handling of IT supported and ICT-enabled education through EduSat; and viii) ensuring inclusive integrated education for the differently abled.

One of the greatest advantages of EduSat supported networks, due to their fast and extensive reach is providing access to some of the best teachers and teaching processes for a very large target group of learners. This will significantly enhance the quality of education. Thus, majority of the schools, BRCs and CRCs located in different parts of the district were connected with EduSat network. A few locations in adjoining districts of neighboring Hindi speaking states were also connected for the project.

6.1.2 Network Provided by ISRO

The network provided by ISRO for wider dissemination in the Sidhi district are; i) 700 Receive Only Terminals (ROTs) Sidhi District; ii) 9 Satellite Interactive Terminals (SITs) in Sidhi for Teacher Training (8 BRCs and DIET); iii) 3 SITs (one each in three adjoining districts of other states); iv) One Hub to support the network at Prantiya Shisha Mahavidyalaya, Jabalpur.

The pilot project has been formally inaugurated by the Hon'ble HRD Minister on Dec. 17, 2005 from EMPC, IGNOU, New Delhi. The Hub (teaching end) for transmission through EDUSAT at PSM, Jabalpur and SIT at DIET, Sidhi were inaugurated on the same day.

6.1.3 Orientation of Teachers

DEP-SSA, IGNOU has organized ten orientation programmes for the elementary schoolteachers on utilization of EduSat capabilities during September 2005 to March 2006. These orientation programmes were organized in collaboration with Regional Centre, IGNOU, Jabalpur, Rajya Shiksha Kendra, Bhopal.

The main objectives of the orientation programme were to, orient teachers in teaching through EDUSAT and their role responsibility in facilitating children's learning i.e. to make them prepare for tele-teaching and how to act as an ideal facilitator during transmission through EduSat. Besides this, certain topics which were covered during the orientation are; i) ICT-enabled and ICT-supported education in the concept and need; ii) EduSat: its characteristics and capabilities; iii) project implementation, monitoring and feedback; iv) role and responsibilities of teachers in the project; v) designing of tele material, tele teaching; and vi) learning from interactive multimedia CDs and concept of collaborative education.

A group of 50 teachers were selected for intensive training in teaching (live) through EduSat. Teachers were trained on the development of e-content and its presentation through television (studio presentation). Although EduSat is used as a medium for the training/education of teachers, it raises several questions with regard to professional development of teachers for quality elementary education.

6.1.4 Research Questions

The study aims to answer the following

i) Do the teachers have favorable perceptions towards teaching through EduSat in relation to; i) acceptance of technology; ii) readiness to use technology; iii) access, feasibility and viability; iv) teaching–learning process adopted in the technology; v) interaction pattern both at learning and teaching end; vi) adequacy of content coverage; vii) presentation style including use of language and TLM; and viii) communication skill?

ii) Does the teaching through EduSat help in professional development of teachers in relation to i) improvement of subject matter; ii) teaching-learning technique; iii) classroom management; Iv) understanding group behaviour; and v) modification of teaching behaviour.

iii) Does the teacher face any problems (academic and administrative) during teaching and learning through EduSat?

iv) How can EDUSAT programme be made more effective for providing quality elementary education?

6.2 Objectives of the Study

The following objectives have been set forth for the present study:

i) To study the effectiveness of technology (teleconferencing) on professional development of teachers.

ii) To study the effectiveness of EduSat on the academic achievement of children at primary grade.

iii) To study the perception of teachers and other functionaries on teaching and learning through EduSat

iv) To study the effectiveness of EduSat for the professional development of teachers.

v) To suggest measures for further improvement of transmission through EduSat.

6.2.1 Rationale of the Study

In the past though several studies have been conducted to study the effectiveness of ICTs. Evaluation of a study on ICT (teleconferencing) in non-formal education indicates that the viewers find the programme interesting and practically useful in their day-to-day activities. Viewers opined that the programme helped them to: i) improve their knowledge (55 percent); ii) spend their leisure profitably (41 percent); and iii) find opportunity for self-employment (24 percent) (Jayatillike, B.G. 2001). Interactive communication using satellite and long distance telephone links contributed to the knowledge gain of the participants and conceptual understanding of participants improved significantly (Trivedi, 1998). Perceptions and reactions towards using teleconferencing as a mode of instruction were generally favourable; participants said that regular use of teleconferencing in future would depend upon improvement in timing, access to telephonic facilities, and high quality of programme content.

No study has been conducted so far to find out the effectiveness of EduSat on professional competency/ development of teachers. So, in the present context, it was felt essential to study the effectiveness of EduSat with regard to professional development of elementary schoolteachers. EduSat is one of the emerging technologies in the field of ICT and is being used in the field of elementary education for providing quality teaching-learning input. Professional development of teacher is one of the prime concerns of EduSat network. Hence, it was decided to undertake this study exclusively with regard to professional development of teachers.

6.3 Collection of Data and its Treatment

Two new sets of questionnaire and one interview schedule were developed and employed for assessing the professional development of elementary schoolteachers and their perception towards EduSat technology. At the same time a focus group discussion was organized to collect relevant qualitative data to supplement the quantitative information obtained through questionnaire. For collection of data and from sample schools of different blocks of Sidhi district, necessary permission of district project coordinators was sought. Block Resource Centre coordinators and heads of the selected schools were contacted on the spot. The task of collection was accomplished with the help of two teacher educators from DIET, Sidhi. The teacher educators were given a short orientation as regards their activities and responsibilities during the time of data collection. The questionnaire was supplied to sample teachers through teacher educators personally. Purpose of the study was explained to them. General instructions with regard to responding the items were thoroughly explained. Each sample respondent was requested to respond all items sincerely. Respondents were assured that the responses would be kept strictly confidential.

Interviews of BRCC and teachers were taken during field visit, with the pre-designed interview schedule by the researcher and two teacher educators. Views, reactions, perception and suggestions were collected from sample respondents through face-to-face interaction.

6.3.1 Data Treatment

The data were analyzed with a view to assessing the current status of elementary teachers of Sidhi district of Madhya Pradesh on professional competency and their perception towards the EduSat technology through questionnaire, interview schedule and FGD. For the above purpose, the statistical technique Chi-square test, and critical ratio were used. The qualitative data (through interview schedule and FGD) were systematically presented to reflect various aspects related to the contribution of EduSat on professional development of teachers and perception of various stakeholders on these aspects.

Necessary rapport was established through personal contacts. In organizing Focus Group Discussion at DIET, Sidhi a thorough discussion was made with the principal, DIET and other teacher educators, regarding the modus operandi of the FGD. Four teacher educators were requested to act as facilitators in four different groups during FGD. Necessary information was given to facilitators regarding their roles and responsibilities during FGD to make the discussion fruitful.

6.4 Major Findings

The findings of the study have been presented systematically in the following sections

Section A: Findings Pertaining to Comparison of the Perception of SSA Functionaries on Effectiveness of Teleconferencing for Professional Development of Teachers

Section B: Findings Pertaining to Comparison of the Performance of Children on Academic Achievement in the ROT and NON -ROT Schools of Sidhi District

Section C: Findings Pertaining to the Perception of Teachers on Quality of Transmission of EDUSAT programme

Section D: Findings Pertaining to the professional Development of Teachers through EduSat Transmission

Section E: Finding pertaining to Focus Group Discussion (FGD)

6.4.1 Section A: Findings Pertaining to Comparison of the Perception of SSA Functionaries on Effectiveness of Teleconferencing for Professional Development of Teachers

The analysis of the present study has yielded some significant findings. Major findings have been discussed under the following headings with regard to inter-state comparison on various aspects of teleconferencing.

I. Technology Related Issues of Teleconferencing:

SSA functionaries of Orissa and Rajasthan vary significantly from one another with regard to their opinion on clarity of visuals and sound of teleconferencing. 84.8% of SSA functionaries of Rajasthan favoured it against 71.1% of those from Orissa. With regard to the accessibility of technology, 97.9% of the functionaries from Orissa supported it against 82.4% from Rajasthan. A very low percentage of teachers, BRC and CRC functionaries of Orissa (3.5%) and Rajasthan (1.7%) did not respond on the usability aspect of teleconferencing.

II. Content and Presentation Aspects of Teleconferencing

There is a significant difference between the responses of SSA functionaries of Orissa and those of Rajasthan with regard to explanation of the content. (C.R. = 2.29) and logical and sequential organization of content (C.R. = 2.59) by the resource person. However, on all other aspects though there exist some differences they are not significant; and. responses of SSA functionaries of Orissa are significantly higher than those of their counterparts from Rajasthan with regard to explanation of content (C.R. = 2.91) as well as logical and sequential organization of content (C.R. = 2.59). This implies that this intervention is not equally effective with regard to certain aspects to both the groups of respondents.

III. Design of Teleconferencing Programme

Functionaries from Orissa as well as Rajasthan did not differ significantly on many aspects of the design of teleconferencing programme except on issues related to adequacy of duration of sessions (C.R. =3.62), use of visuals (C.R. = 4.14), time for which visuals are shown (C.R. = 2.71) and need ability of text/captions. (C.R. = 3.06); and almost one-third (36.6%) of SSA functionaries of Orissa disagreed on the adequacy of the duration of teleconferencing sessions than their counterparts (10.3%) from Rajasthan and the difference is significant (C.R. = 2.59). This applies as well to the time for which visuals were shown.

IV. Interaction during Teleconferencing

The difference in responses of SSA functionaries of Orissa and those of Rajasthan with regard to adequacy of the interaction with resource persons is significant (C.R. = 3.73). About 88% of SSA functionaries of Rajasthan against 69% of Orissa felt that his intervention was adequate; and as regard to the clarification of doubt, 92.5% of SSA functionaries of Orissa supported it against 81.3% from Rajasthan and the difference is significant (C.R. = 2.56). On all other aspects related to interaction during teleconferencing programme, there was no significant difference between the responses from these two states

V. Teachers' Responses on Different Aspects of Teleconferencing

Significant differences were found on different aspects of teleconferencing: i) teleconferencing helps in handling classroom problems/situations effectively (C.R. 4.68); ii) teleconferencing helps increase retention of children in the classroom (C.R. 4.34); iii) teleconferencing equips the teacher better to contribute towards the goals of SSA (C.R. = 3.58). More elementary schoolteachers of Rajasthan agreed on the aspects than their counterparts from Orissa and the differences were significant. A higher percentage of elementary schoolteachers belonging to Orissa had a favourable view on effective organization of content of teaching learning than that of Rajasthan and the difference is significant (C.R.=3.72). The following differences in responses were also significant: inclusive education (C.R. =3.72) and appreciating issues of girls' education (C.R=3.40).

VI. Responses of BRC and CRC Functionaries on Different Aspect of Teleconferencing

It was noticed that the percentage of favourable responses of BRC and CRC functionaries of Rajasthan is on the higher side than that of their counterparts from Orissa and the difference is significant on all aspects of teleconferencing except on issues related to effectiveness of teleconferencing for teacher training programme (C.R. = 0.99). Very low percentage of BRC and CRC functionaries (39.3%) of Orissa and Rajasthan (31.3%) agreed that teleconferencing is an effective medium for training of teachers. A sizeable percentage of BRC and CRC functionaries from both the states Orissa (55.9%) and of Rajasthan (63.7%) did not respond on the effectiveness of teleconferencing for teacher training purposes; and very low percentage of BRC and CRC functionaries (4.8%) from Orissa and also from Rajasthan completely disagreed that teleconferencing is an effective medium for teacher training programmes.

VII. Responses of Teachers, BRC and CRC Functionaries on Various Aspects of Teleconferencing

Though there exists a number of differences of opinion between the SSA functionaries of Orissa and of Rajasthan on different issues related to teleconferencing these differences are not significant except with regard to responses of BRC and CRC functionaries. There is no significant difference between the responses of SSA functionaries from Orissa and those from Rajasthan; it can be said that respondents from both the states agree in equal measure about the effectiveness of teleconferencing.

6.4.2 Section B: Findings Pertaining to Comparison of the Performance of Children on Academic Achievement in the ROT and NON -ROT Schools of Sidhi District

I. Average Performance of Children

- It is found that the overall average achievement level of children of Std V of ROT and NON-ROT schools of Sidhi district is at comparable level i.e. both children of both categories of schools are nearly at the same level (M% = 46.36 for ROT schools and 46.78 for NON-ROT schools).
- Under many subgroups the Mean percentage of children of Std V of ROT schools are higher like General Girls, General Boys + Girls, SC Boys, ST Boys, OBC Boys, OBC Girls and OBC Boys + Girls than their counterparts of NON-ROT schools. But these differences are not statistically significant.
- On the basis of overall comparison, it is found that in Std III Mean percentage of children of ROT schools

(39.62) are higher than NON-ROT schools (37.46). It equally holds good for Boys (M% of ROT school 42.16 and NON-ROT school 41.96) and Girls (M% of ROT Schools 37.08 and NON-ROT schools 32.95) as well.

II Performance of children in Hindi

- In case of boys of Class V, there is no significant difference between the Mean achievement in Hindi of ROT and NON-ROT schools but in case of girls, the difference is significant and goes in favour of children of NON-ROT schools. The Mean percentage of children of NON-ROT school is higher than that of their ROT counterparts.
- In case of all other subgroups like General, SC, ST, OBC also the Mean percentage of children of Class V is higher for children of NON-ROT schools.
- Mean percentage of children of Class III in Hindi of ROT schools are lower than their counterparts of NON-ROT schools under all groups and subgroups except General Boys and OBC Girls. But in none of the groups and subgroups, it is found to be significant on the basis of observed critical ratio values.
- Comparison of the Mean achievement of children from ROT and NON-ROT schools of each standard shows that there exists a difference between the achievement level of children but it is surprising to note that though the differences are not significant yet they go in favour of children of NON-ROT schools.

III Performance of Children in English

- Comparison of the Mean achievement of children of Std V in English between ROT and NON-ROT schools Sidhi district shows that children of ROT schools perform better (higher mean percentage) than NON-ROT counterparts. This hold good in case of all groups like General, SC, ST and OBC as well. Similar is the situation with regard to certain subgroup like General Girls, SC Boys, SC girls, ST girls and OBC Girls.

- This is no significant difference between the Mean percentage of children of Std III in English belonging to ROT and NON-ROT schools of Sidhi district but it goes in favour of children of ROT schools under all groups and subgroups except in case of SC girls, ST boys and ST girls.
- In English performance of children under ROT schools is found to be higher than that of NON-ROT schools in both class III and as well as Class V.

IV Performance of Children in EVS

- Mean percentage of Girls (M=50.53) and Boys + Girls (M=50.46) of Std V in ROT schools is more than that of their counterparts belonging to NON-ROT schools in EVS but in case of boys (M=50.90) of Std V in ROT schools, it is lower than their counterparts of NON-ROT schools.
- In certain subgroups under ROT schools like Gen. Girls (M=53.14), Gen. Boys + Girls (M=52.62), ST Girls (50.4) OBC Boys (M=58.39) OBC Girls (M=56.88) and OBC Boys +girls (M=57.62) the Mean percentage is higher in comparison to their NON-ROT counterparts.
- In case of children of Std III Mean percentage of children of ROT schools are higher than Non ROT

counterparts except under certain subgroups like SC girls ST boys and OBC boys.

- In ROT schools achievements of Boys and Girls of Std III and Girls of Std V in EVS and in other subgroups as well are higher than their NON-ROT counterparts which clearly reflect the efficacy of the transmission through EduSat.

V Performance of Children in Mathematics

- It is found that the Mean percentage of children in mathematics under ROT schools of Sidhi district is higher that that of their NON-ROT schools counterparts. This hold good in case of Boys, Girls and under certain subgroups like Gen. Boys, ST boys, ST girls, OBC boys and OBC girls. Though the differences are not statistically significant yet they go in favor of children of ROT schools.
- The Mean percentage of children of class III in mathematics is higher in case of general and OBC category belonging to ROT schools but in case of SC and ST children the Mean percentage of NON-ROT schoolchildren is higher except for SC girls.
- There is no significant difference between the Mean percentage of children of class III belonging to ROT and NON-ROT schools of Sidhi district but in very few cases it goes in favor of children of ROT schools i.e. Gen. Boys (Mean per cent = 49.79) Gen. Girls (Mean per cent =38.2), Gen. Boys+Girls (Mean per cent =44), SC Boys (Mean per cent =39.7), ST Girls (Mean percent =35.07), ST Boys+Girls (Mean percent =37.14), OBC Girls (Mean percent = 38.19) etc.

6.4.3 SECTION C: Findings pertaining to the Perception of Teachers on Quality of Transmission of EduSat Programme

- More than 50 percent of teachers agreed that the topic of transmission was useful for their professional development and duration of the transmission on each topic was sufficient. But only 23.75 percent teachers agreed that language used by the tele-teachers was simple and understandable.
- About 55-60 percent of teachers did not agree that tele-teachers provide sufficient activities for teachers and develop interactive environment during presentation. Only 15-20 per cent teachers agreed on it whereas 20-30 per cent teachers did not respond to these important issues.
- On the aspect related to preparation of tele-teacher for presentation of topic with suitable examples and illustration, it was found that only 35-40 percent teachers agreed, whereas more than 30 pe cent of teachers did not respond.
- 57.5 per cent teachers were facing difficulties from presentation of tele-teachers and only 30-40 percent teachers agreed that the standard of presentation was appropriate and overall quality presentation was satisfactory.
- It was found that only 10 percent of teachers were involved in discussion after the transmission but 50 percent of teachers do not agree on it and 30 percent teachers did not respond to it.
- A significant difference was found between the responses of teachers with regard to receiving of prior

information about the topic (Y^2 = 11.07**) usefulness (Y^2 = 22.35**) and relevance of the topic (Y^2 = 8.4*) for professional development, activities provided by tele-teachers (Y^2 = 19.56**) developing interactive environment during presentation (Y^2 = 20.09**) and discussion made by teachers during post-transmission (Y^2 = 30.27**)

6.4.4 Section D: Findings Pertaining to the Professional Development of Teachers through EduSat Transmission

- Larger percentage of teachers (about 57.67 percent) felt that transmission of EduSat focuses on making teaching.-learning process more effective, emphasizes on effective organization of interaction sessions during the teaching-learning process and relates to work with other staff members, parents and community together whereas only 35-40 percent teachers agreed that it explains strategies for effective use of TLMs and tips for use of ICTs for making teaching-learning process realistic and interesting.
- Most of the teachers (more than 55 percent) disagreed on various aspects of the organization of the teaching-learning process like (i) Systematic Organization of Instructional Objectives (58.75 percent) (ii) Appropriate selection of teaching-learning material (55.00 percent); (iii) Sequential presentation of content (67.5 percent); and (iv) Development of suitable text items for evaluation (77.5 per cent) but about 51.25 percent of teachers agreed on meaningful sequencing of content and learning activities.
- More than 50.00 percent of teachers agreed on fruitful

contribution of EduSat to aspects related to development of managerial skills like motivating children and development of potential to work in a team, effective management of time for curricular and co-curricular activities, appropriate and effective use of human resources for optimum development of children and developing technique of classroom management etc.

- Perception of teachers on various issues related to evaluation and monitoring of curricular and co-curricular aspects was very poor as larger percentage of teachers disagreed on certain crucial issues like (i) measuring of behaviour outcome of children on and around the classroom (73.75 per cent); (ii) construction of tools and techniques for assessing learning outcomes (71.25 percent); (iii) monitoring progress of student and perception of teacher (7.5 per cent); and (iv) measure to diagnose difficulties of children (80.00 percent).
- Though about 65.00 per cent of teachers agreed that EduSat transmission provides fundamental aspects related to skillful use of the concept of measurement and evaluation, 35 percent of teachers disagreed on it as well.
- It was found that most of the teachers (72.5 percent) felt that EduSat transmission focuses on academic as well as administrative aspects for professional development but 27.5 percent of teachers disagreed on it.
- With regard to overall personality development of teachers and their perception as a profession, it was found that only 28.75 percent teachers agreed on it whereas remaining (71.25 percent) disagreed on this aspect.

- There is no significant difference between the responses of teachers with regard to (i) explanation of strategies of using communication aids; (ii) tips to use ICTs; (iii) training through EduSat relating work with colleagues, parents and community; (iv) systematic organization of instructional objectives; (v) meaningful sequencing of content and learning activities; (vi) appropriate selection of teaching-learning material; (vii) techniques on classroom management, (viii) appropriate and effective use of human resources; (ix) skill for motivating children; (x) monitoring children's progress and their own performance; (xi) scope for all round development of children and teaching process by effective use of technology and (xii) focus on instructional objectives and its outcome.

Average percentage of teachers was in favour of the above contribution of EduSat on the above aspects for the professional development. The divergence in responses (perception) of teachers was marked significant on the basis of chi-square value.

With regard to: i) effective teaching-learning process through EduSat (9.80**); ii) effective organization of interactive session (4.2*); iii) appropriate and sequential presentation of content (9.90**); iv) development of suitable text items for evaluation (24.20**); v) effective management of time for curricular and co-curricular activities (9.80**); vi); skillful use of the concept of measurement and evaluation (7.20**), ii) measurement of behavioural outcome of children (18.04**); (iv) construction of tools and techniques (14.44**); (v) measure to diagnose difficulties of children (28.8**); (vi) opportunity for developing curiosity of teachers to use ICTs for classroom-teaching-learning process; and (vii) change in overall personality and perception of teachers (8.45**)

6.4.5 Section E: Findings pertaining to Focus Group Discussion (FGD)

I. First Phase FGD

- Transmission needs to be focused on subject, content and class for which it is meant; presentation of content should not deviate from normal transactional strategy. It must correspond to the level of children and academic calendar as well. More emphasis should be given on difficult and problematic issues related to content and its presentation.
- Teachers at learning end do not carry our pre and post-transmission discussion with children for comprehensive clarity on the content.
- The difficult topic and concepts of a particular subject may be repeated again and again to clear the understanding of children. At the same time pedagogical part may also be highlighted for the benefit of teachers.
- New methods with adequate innovation are implemented in delivering the lesson so as to make it interesting and effective. Teachers of all elementary level should be given training on how to facilitate the teaching-learning process during transmission. Active involvement of teachers plays a major role in developing interest and curiosity of learners.
- Tele-teachers do not focus on local dialect, which creates problem in understanding as the target group is from typical rural background.

- Provision should be made by authorities to orient one/ two persons from local community on maintenance of ROTs and accountability should be fixed on them so that teachers, and BRC/CRC functionaries can spare more time on academic activities.
- District administrators should make a random check/ supervision at least once in a month, so as to make the block authority alert and boost the morality of teachers.
- Teachers working in primary and elementary schools should be free from non-academic activities, so that they can use their time for academic improvement of children and plan constructively for overall development of teaching-learning processes with the help of EduSat transmission.
- Record of each and every telecast programme should be maintained properly at the learning end to provide feedback for improvement in future; but we teachers do not get enough time for it due to inadequate number of teachers at school.
- No ROT is installed at BRCs and CRCs level, the presence of which is an essential requirement for effective monitoring.
- Provision should be made from district authority to supervise the programme monthly and submit the report to state level authorities, but no adequate steps have been taken up so far.
- Headmasters of elementary school, where adequate staff is available, should be given responsibility to send their teachers for monitoring nearby schools.
- Detailed programme schedule indicating class, subject and topic should be circulated well in advance to all

schools for information and necessary action but unfortunately we did not get it in time.

- At each block, a monitoring team is constituted for supervising, visiting schools during transmission period; they need to be empowered to send confidential reports directly to state authorities.
- Each BRCC must send a supervisory report of at least one school in a day. It should be made compulsory.
- VEC may be given authority to monitor the programme of EduSat so that regularity can be expected to some extent.

II Second Phase FGD

- DIET functionaries are not involved in monitoring, supervision and assessment of EduSat transmission in Sidhi district, which is an unfortunate situation with regard to improvement of EduSat programme.
- More emphasis is given on sequential development of content and its systematic presentation according to level of children as suggested by teacher educators.
- Varieties of activities are not incorporated in presenting the difficult content and scope for revision and recapitulation must be kept open for children.
- Pre and post-transmission activity is important for enhancing academic performance of children. So in every school the teacher concerned may be entrusted with the responsibility to look into the EduSat activities, its feedback and plan for its remedial activity etc.
- BRCCs hardly supervises the school during transmission

- A tele-teacher simply uses lecture method in many cases for presentation of topic; they hardly follow demonstration and other innovation sometimes commit mistakes in presentation particularly in teaching mathematics and science topics
- Teachers of elementary school hardly watch the programme transmitted on Saturday.
- Many teachers felt it is like normal classroom teaching; they do not find any interaction and innovative techniques related to pedagogy.
- State and district administration hardly take any measure for inspection, supervision, monitoring for improving the quality of EDUSAT program.
- Most of the ROTs are not in functional condition but higher authorities remain silent about it; even where the ROT and TV sets had been stolen no action has been initiated so far.
- Language used by tele-teachers during presentation is a hurdle for the students as the schools are in rural belt; so they prefer local dialect rather than common language.

6.5 Educational Implications

The findings of the present study have implications for planning strategies in general and also district-wise, focusing on transmission of EduSat, quality of tele-teaching and various aspects related to professional development of elementary schoolteachers.

One of the objectives of the present study was to examine the effectiveness of Information Communication Technologies (Teleconferencing) on professional development of SSA functionaries. For the purpose, a trend analysis has been made in terms of different indicators of professional development as discussed in Chapter II. The analysis, in general, indicates that we are steadily and surely making consistent progress towards the effective use of teleconferencing, but our specific observation based on the present study required strategic planning and implication.

In the state of Orissa and Rajasthan, the increase in use of teleconferencing for capacity building of teachers, BRCCs, CRCCs and the SSA functionaries was quite encouraging. But measures need to be taken up to develop facilities at learning ends and improve the quality of transmission (content). The technical support from DEP-SSA, IGNOU may be taken for improving the quality of transmission and experts participating from area concerned should be invited from national level in collaboration with DEP-SSA. Orientation for anchorperson and facilitator may be organized at state level. Pre and post-teleconferencing discussion may be organized for effective and meaningful transmission. It is advisable that feedback study be undertaken to improve the programme time to time on the basis of the need of local teachers and other target group. Since all the sample districts were found having inadequate essential facilities in the areas of seating arrangement, telephone, fax, proper audio facilities, and initiative may be undertaken to mobilize district authorities for additional resources in order to ward off the financial crunch and to make available the funds for the above purpose. The teachers, BRCCs, CRCCs may be empowered to managerial responsibility at their level. The number of women teachers participating in teleconferencing is relatively small in all most all districts of Orissa and Rajasthan. More number of women teachers should be provided an opportunity so that their services could be utilized to improve the quality of elementary education in our country. Steps may be taken to allow more and more newly recruited teachers to attend the teleconferencing programme from remote areas to improve their professional standard. Provision may be made to provide learning centers at block level to cover a large number of teachers and to meet the basic needs of teachers working in inaccessible areas.

With regard to the objective of the study related to academic achievement of children (when taught through technology (EDUSAT), an analysis has been made in terms of gender and caste. The analysis indicates a mixed result (effectiveness of EduSat on academic performance of children). While establishing the validity of EduSat intervention, the findings suggest that as children move from early grades to upper classes in primary schools, probably a more direct control, continuous monitoring and follow up is essential even up to class V.

The observations regarding the prominence of the element of contextuality during the study has also been confirmed through the findings of the present study by way of comparing the children of ROT and NON-ROT schools on their achievement (i.e. Hindi, English, EVS and Mathematics) on the competency-based tests. For instance, significant achievement gains have been noticed in case of ROT schools for class V and III children in many cases. These suggest that interventions through ROT (EduSat transmission) have had a mixed impact; on the contrary, significant losses can be observed in the achievement of mathematics and English for Class III and V. All these obviously warrant block specific educational plans and varied interventions for individual blocks to cater to the specific needs. This in turns indirectly reflects the efficacy of the professional efficiency of teachers working at various levels (primary and elementary) of Sidhi district.

The main objective of the study was to analyze the effectiveness of EduSat on the professional development of elementary schoolteachers. On the basis of the trend analysis it was found that teachers working at elementary level of Sidhi district have opened their minds with regard to improving their efficacy on the teaching-learning process. They are found to be more enthusiastic in knowing things from EduSat transmission, which is a positive indicator on the part of professional improvement. A thorough planning is needed for providing quality input to teachers. Teachers in general need interaction for clarifying their doubts but unfortunately EduSat technology is not able to provide it at present. A systematic discussion regarding the topic of transmission can enhance the interest of teachers to get themselves actively watch and/participate in EDUSAT programme. The following intervention strategies have been proposed for the purpose.

- Teachers awareness towards professional development, professional competencies should be increased.
- Physical facilities for adequate seating arrangement and providing adequate teachers are essential for making the objective of EduSat a success.
- ROT facilities may be provided in all schools on a large scale.
- Adequate provision should be made for the maintenance and repair of ROT and TV sets from time to time, so that teachers and children do not lose the continuity.

- Management of the ROT sets and TV sets should be in the hands of community.
- Recurrent orientation/training should be provided to teachers relating to use of technology and its effective implementation for improving the quality of education.
- Topic for transmission should be designed to create interest in children and teachers with adequate examples, illustrations and challenging activities.
- Instructional material should be developed in tribal language at the initial stage, with arrangements for switching over to the regional language.
- In-service teachers training programme, joyful learning and capacity building at different level must be emphasized for developing confidence level of teachers.
- Local teachers must be given an opportunity to work as tele-teachers with adequate training so that a spirit of competitiveness can be developed among teachers working in rural schools.
- Activity-based instruction must be designed for transmission through EduSat.

Findings relating to the present study clearly indicate that EduSat transmission is able to attract the attention of teachers towards the effective use of technology for making classroom teaching-learning process more interactive and fruitful. There is a need to understand the needs of teachers working in rural schools and their problems as well. Content of transmission should focus on classroom dynamics and selection of teaching-learning material and activity for classroom transaction effectively. This brings into focus a planning strategy in EduSat that teachers be oriented, monitored as well as academically supervised during teaching by necessary supervisory functionaries for on the spot remedy of the situation, rather than routine in-service training which is going on in education without follow-up mechanism since inception. The above observations, generalization and implications are also applicable for developing professional efficiency of elementary schoolteachers. This strategy will eventually remove the disparity, whatever exists either due to real geographical factors, instructional deficiency, or from within organization mechanism.

6.6 Recommendations

The following recommendations may be considered for improving the effectiveness of EduSat transmission.

- Presentation of content should be made systematic, sequential to make it more effective and interesting.
- Appropriate planning of tele-lessons and selection of competent tele-teachers should be given priority to make it more interactive and child-centered.
- Use of local dialects, proper communication aids, is prerequisite for attracting the attention of primary school children.
- In addition to content-based programme, it is essential to transmit value based, entertainment-based, physical education-based programme from time to time in the form of fillers.
- Transmission for teachers needs to be thematic-based and activity-based so that teachers working at the elementary level can take it as a challenge rather than watching it for entertainment.
- The subject teacher needs to maintain a record of transmission of content and discuss it with children immediately after the transmission is over.

- Regular monitoring and supervision of the EduSat transmission (both at teaching and learning ends) be undertaken.
- VECs may be assigned the responsibility to provide the benefit of transmission to community members, for which awareness-based programmes may be transmitted on Sundays and other holidays.
- Recurrent training/orientation in ICTs particularly utilization of EduSat facilities may be organized for teachers, parents, VECs and community members.

6.7 Suggestions for Further Research

In the light of the present study the following suggestions are offered for further research:

i) The study may be replicated on larger samples covering other schools of Sidhi district and schools from Sonebhadra district of UP, Vaishali district of Bihar and Koria district of Chhatisgarh.

ii) Factors related to home, school might be studied which contributes to professional development of teachers.

iii) Refinement of questionnaire on professional development/competency may be attempted in a more precise manner.

iv) Higher statistical techniques like Factor Analysis may be used for better analysis and interpretation of data.

v) Focus Group Discussions may be organized more comprehensively to collect qualitative data related to professionalism of elementary schoolteachers.

vi) The findings of the study need further cross validation.

❖ ❖ ❖

Appendix

Dear friends,

You have been watching the EDUSAT transmission over last one year. These programmes were designed and developed with the objectives of improving your teaching competencies and enabling you to become a better teacher. You know that professional development of teachers is an essential requirement for quality elementary education. Through EDUSAT attempt has been taken to provide training/orientation to teachers in addition to providing quality teaching to children. In order to evaluate the effectiveness of this EDUSAT transmission on your professional development, a study has been undertaken. Your responses to the questions that follow in the sections below will help us to improve the quality of transmission through EDUSAT. Please do not hesitate to express your honest opinion. Your responses will be kept confidence and will be used for research purpose only.

The questionnaire has three sections. Section A contains personal information. Section B contains your perception towards quality of transmission of EDUSAT programme and Section C contains the effectiveness of EDUSAT transmission in improving your professional efficiency as a teacher.

Section A: Personal Information for all the Respondents

1. Name :

2. Age :

3. Sex : Male/Female

4. Total Experience (in years) :

5. School Name :

6. CRC Name :

7. Block Name :

8. District Name :

9. State Name :

Section B: Perception of Teachers on Quality of Transmission through EDUSAT

IB	*Transmission Related Issues:*	*Agree*	*Disagree*	*No Response*
1.	I received the information about the topic to be transmitted in advance.	☐	☐	☐
2.	I found the topic relevant for professional development.	☐	☐	☐
3.	I found the topic useful for professional development	☐	☐	☐
4.	Tele teachers used clear and simple language which were understandable	☐	☐	☐
5.	Duration of transmission for each topic was sufficient			

IIB	*Performance of Tele-Teachers:*	*Agree*	*Disagree*	*No Response*
1.	Tele teachers present and explain the lesson with thorough preparation.	☐	☐	☐
2.	Tele teachers explained the content with many activities.	☐	☐	☐

3.	Tele teachers explained the content with suitable examples and illustrations.	☐	☐	☐
4.	I was getting sufficient activity from tele-teachers.	☐	☐	☐
5.	Tele-teachers developed interactive environment during teaching-learning process.	☐	☐	☐
IIIB	*Teaching-Learning Process through EDUSAT*	*Agree*	*Disagree*	*No Response*
1.	I faced difficulties from the presentation of tele-teachers.	☐	☐	☐
2.	I found the tele-teachers commits common mistakes.	☐	☐	☐
3.	I found the level of presentation quite appropriate	☐	☐	☐
4.	I found the overall quality of presentation satisfactory.	☐	☐	☐
5.	My colleagues developed interest towards EduSat programme.	☐	☐	☐
6.	The sessions prompted me to interact with my colleagues	☐	☐	☐

Section C: Effectiveness of EDUSAT Professional Development of Elementary School Teachers.

IC	*Issue Related to Development of Communication Skills*	*Agree*	*Disagree*	*No Response*
1.	Provide clues/tips for making teaching-learning process more effective.	☐	☐	☐
2.	Emphasizes on effective organization of interactive session during teaching learning process.	☐	☐	☐
3.	Explain strategies of using communication aids for making teaching learning process effective.	☐	☐	☐
4.	Developed potentiality of teachers to use ICTs in classroom.	☐	☐	☐
5.	Training through EduSat relate to and work with colleagues and other members.	☐	☐	☐

IIC	*Issue Related to Organization of Teaching Learning Process*	*Agree*	*Disagree*	*No Response*
1.	Focus on organization of instructional objectives systematically.	☐	☐	☐

2.	Concentrate on logical sequencing of content and learning activities meaningfully.	☐	☐	☐
3.	Orient in selection of teaching-learning materials and its effective transaction in classroom.	☐	☐	☐
4.	Provide opportunity of practice on presenting the content sequentially and appropriately.	☐	☐	☐
5.	Focus on development of suitable text items for evaluation.	☐	☐	☐
IIIC	*Issue Related to Management of Curricular and Co-curricular Activities:*	*Agree*	*Disagree*	*No Response*
1.	Focus on development of managerial skills to motivate students and work in a team.	☐	☐	☐
2.	Develop motivation on effective organizational capacities.	☐	☐	☐
3.	Emphasizes on effective management of time for curricular and co-curricular activities.	☐	☐	☐

		Agree	Disagree	No Response
4.	Concentrate on using human resources appropriately and effectively for optimum development.	☐	☐	☐
5.	Provide opportunity to concentrate on effective implementation of technology in classroom.	☐	☐	☐
IVC	*Issue Related to Evaluation and Monitoring*	*Agree*	*Disagree*	*No Response*
1.	Help in developing skill of measurement and evaluation in and outside the classroom.	☐	☐	☐
2.	Focuses on behavioural outcome of children.	☐	☐	☐
3.	Provide adequate knowledge from construction of hints and techniques for assessment of evaluation.	☐	☐	☐
4.	Emphasizes on monitoring the progress of children as well as their own performance.	☐	☐	☐
5.	Suggest measures to diagnose difficulties of children.	☐	☐	☐

VC	*Issue Related to Personal Attitudes*	*Agree*	*Disagree*	*No Response*
1.	Provide maximum opportunities for developing interest and curiosity in using ICTs.	☐	☐	☐
2.	Provide scopes for all round development of children and teaching profession	☐	☐	☐
3.	Focuses on academic and administrative aspects for professional improvement	☐	☐	☐
4.	Develop interest to focus on instructional objectives and its outcome.	☐	☐	☐
5.	Bring a change in overall personality and perception of teachers as a professional.	☐	☐	☐

❖ ❖ ❖

Bibliography

Admar (1996): National Viewership Research Survey on UGC Survey on UGC Countrywide Classroom Programme in India, New Delhi, Consortium for Educational Communication.

Adnanes, M. and Ronning, W.N. (1998): Computer Networks in Education: a Better Way to Learn? Journal of Computer Assisted Learning, 14 (2), 148-157.

Aghi, Mira B. (1977): Impact of Science Education Programmes on SITE Children of Rajasthan, Ahmedabad, Space Applications Centre.

Agrawal, Binod C. (1978): Television Comes to Village: An Evaluation of SITE, Bangalore, Indian Space Research Organization.

Agrawal, Binod C. (1996): Pedagogy of Computer Literacy: An Indian Experience, New Delhi, Concept Publishing Company.

Agrawal, Binod C. (2005): Educational Media in India in *Perceptive on Distance Education : Educational Media in Asia,* Usha V. Reddi and Sanjaya Mishra (Eds.), Voncouver, Commonwealth of Learning.

Barksdale-Ladd, M.A. (1994): Teacher empowerment and literacy instruction in three professional development schools. Journal of Teacher Education, 45 (20), 104-111

Becker, H.J. (1992): Computer-based integrated learning systems in the elementary and middle grades: Critical review and synthesis of evaluation reports. Journal of Educational Computing Research, 8 (1), 1-41.

BECTA (2000): A preliminary report on the relationship between ICT and primary school standards, British Educational Communications and Technology Agency, London

Behera, S.C. (1991): Impact of Educational Television on the Competency of Elementary School Teachers. Ph.D. thesis, Bhubaneshwar, Utkal University.

Buch, M.B. (1991): Fourth Survey of research in Education 1983-88, Volume I and II, New Delhi, NCERT.

Chaudhary, M.M. (1997): The Limits and Challenges of Educational Technology in the Paradigm of Sustainable Development of India, in Educational Technology 2000. A Global Vision for Open and Distance Learning (Conference papers) Singapore (August 15-17). The Commonwealth of Learning.

Chaudhary, S.S, (1991): Teachers Attitude towards School Televisin and Its Relationship with Mass Media Behaviour and Job Satisfaction. Ph.D. thesis, University of Delhi, Delhi

Chaudhary, S. S. and Bansal, K. (2000): Interactive Radio Counseling in Indira Gandhi National Open University – A Study. Journal of Distance Education 15 (2): 37-51, quoted by Sanjay Mishra in his paper op.cit, P.74.

Chaudhary, S.S.and Panda, S. (1997): Education Television: Review of Research, Staff and Educational Development International 1 (2 & 3), 179-187.

Chaudhary, S.S. and Panda, S.(2005): Educational Television and Teleconference in Perspectives on Distance Education : Educational media in Asia, Usha V. Reddi and Sanjaya Mishra (Editors), Vancouver, Commonwealth of Learning: Chapter 7, PP79-95.

CIET (1983 a): A Report on Quick Feedback obtained from the User-Teachers on ETV Programmes in Andhra Pradesh and Orissa, New Delhi, NCERT

CIET (1983b): A Study of the Impact of ETV Programmes on the Children of Class IV and V in Sambalpur District (Orissa), NCERT , New Delhi.

CIET (1992): Use of Educational Television in Andhra Pradesh, NCERT., New Delhi

CIET (1993): A Study on Utilization of ETV Service for the Children and the Teachers at the Primary Level in Puri and Dhenkanal District of Orissa, New Delhi, NCERT.

CIET (1996): A Report on ETV Utilization in maharashtra 1985-86; NCERT (mimeo). New Delhi.

Combs (2000): Assessing the role of educational technology in the teaching and lerning process: a learned perspective, Department of Education, Washington DC, USA

Dash, N.K. (1997): "Reactions of Primary Schol Teachers towards Training through Interactive Television", Indian Journal of Open Learning 6 (1&2): 77-90.

Deal, N. (1995): Is the medium the message? Comparing student perceptions of teacher responses via written and e-mail forms. Paper presented at the annual National Educational Computing Conference, Baltimore, MD. (ERIC Document Reproduction Service No. ED 392 432)

DEP (2002): Effectiveness of Teleconferencing: An Evaluative Study, DEP-DPEP Haryana, IGNOU-NCERT Collaborative Project, New Delhi.

DEP (2003a): Distance Education Initiatives in District Primary Education Progamme (DPEP), INDIA, National Report, New Delhi: An IGNOU, IGNOU-NCERT Collaborative Project (sponsored by Ministry of HRD, Government of India) PP 161-169.

DEP (2003b): Study of Feedback of Teleconference Programme, Distance Education Programme – Maharashtra Prathamik Shikshan Parishad, Mumbai.

DEP-OPEPA (2005): A Report on Feedback Analysis of the content based Radio Programme (Ankur I and Ankur II) in Children's Programme "Kakali" for the target groups under Sarva Shiksha Abhiyan, Bhubaneshwar, Orissa.

Diggs, C.S. (1997): Technology: a key to unlocking at risk students, learning and leading with technology 25 (2), 38-40.

Dimock, K.V. (1996): Building Relationships, Engaging Students: A Naturalistic Study of Classrooms participating in the Electronic Emissary Project. (On-line). Available : http://www.tapr.org/emissary/

Dimock, V. and Boethel, M. (1999): Constructing Knowledge with Technology, Southwest Educational Development Laboratory.

Available: http://www.sedl.org/pubs/tec27/18.html

Ferneding-Lenert, K.F. and Harris, J.B. (1994): Redefining expertise and reallocating roles in text-based asynchronous teaching/learning environments. Machine Mediated Learning, 4 (2/3), 129-148.

Forcheri, P. and Monfind, M.T. (2000): ICT as a tool for learning to learn. In Watson, D.M. and Downes, T.

(Eds.) Comunication and Networking in Education, Boston, MA : Kluwer Academic.

Gangappa,K and Chandraiah, E (2004): Responses of Learner to Technology-based Learning in ODL : A Case Study of Dr. B.R. Ambedkar Open University in *Indian Journal of Open Learning :* 13 (1), January, New Delhi, IGNOU, PP 87-96.

Goel, D.R. and et.al; (2003): ICT in Education : Changes and Challenges, in ICT in Education, Vadodara : Centre for Advanced Study in Education, The M.S. University of Baroda, pp 1-14.

Gupta, N.K. (2003a): Potentials of Radio Programme, Gyankalash for Teaches – Himachal Pradesh Experience, The Primary Teacher, October 2003, pp 48-56, New Delhi, NCERT.

Gupta, N.K. (2003b): Abhiprerana, DEP-DPEP, New Delhi, IGNOU.

Gupta, N.K. (2003c): Sudent – Gyankalash Radio Programme, New Delhi, DEP-DPEP, IGNOU.

Gupta, N.K. (2004a): Communication through Teleconferencing – An Educational Perspective, a paper submitted to Journal of Indian Education, New Delhi, NCERT.

Gupta, N.K. (2004b): Teleconferencing – Yoyage to Sarva Shiksha Abhiyan, a paper submitted to the Primary Teacher, New Delhi, NCERT.

Gupta, N.K. (2004c): Using Technology for Monitoring Sarva Shiksha Abhiyan – teleconferencing on appraised mission, a paper submitted to NCERT, New Delhi for publication in Journal of Indian Education.

Harasim, L. (1989): On-line education : anew domain. In R. Mason and A. Kaye (Eds.), Mindweave: Communication, Computers and Distance Education (pp.50-62). Oxford : Pergamon Press.

Honey, M., and Henriquez, A. (1996): Union City Interactive Multimedia Education Trial: 1993-95 Summary Reports. CCT Reports Issue No. 3 [On-line] Available : http://www.edc.org/CCT/

Irving, A. (1991): The educational value and use of on-line information services in schools. Computers in Education 17 (3), 213-225

Jegede, O (2000): Using Open and Distance learning Methods in Primary Teacher Education in Nigeria – CDL, World Bank Project.

Jonassen, D.H. (1996): Computers in the Classroom : Mindtools for Critical Thinking. Englewood Cliffs, New Jersey : Prentice-Hall, Inc.

Joshi, Vibha (1988): The Effectiveness of School Television Programes in Science at Secondary School Level. Ph.D. thesis, M.S. University of Baroda, Gujarat

Khan, A.W. (2001): Professional Development with Learning Technologies – paper presented during International Workshop on Information and Communication Technology for Professional Development of Primary Education Personnel, February 14-16, 2001, New Delhi, DEP-DPEP, IGNOU.

Kozma, R. and Ghee, R. (1999): World for Development : Accomplishments & Challenges. Monitoring & Evaluation Annual Report, 1998-99. Menlo Park, CA : SRI International.

Kozma, R.B. (2003): ICT and Educational Reform in Developed and Developing Countries, Centre for Technology in Learning, California, SRI International.

Kulik, J.A. (1994): Meta-Analytic studies of findings on computer-based instruction. In E.L. Baker and H.F. O'Neill (Eds.), Technology Assessment in Education and Training. Hillsdale, NJ: Lawrence Erlbaum Publishers

Leach, I. (1997): Changing Discourse, Transforming Pedagogy: Developing an online community for Teacher Education, Paper presented at the Third European Research Association, Frankfurt Sept. 24-27

Little john, A., Stefani, L and Sclater, N. (1999): Promoting effective use of technology, Pedagogy and the Practicalities: a case study. Active Learning, 11, 27-30.

Loannides, C. (2002): Assimilation of ICT in Schools and Accommodation of School Structures. Five Case Studies. Proceedings of the 3rd International Conference on ICT in Education Samoa Islands : Greece.

Lockheed, M.E. (2001): Impact study of World Links for Development, World Bank International Evaluation Briefs, Geneva.

Lowry, M. et.al; (1994): Electronic discussion groups: using e-mail as an instructional strategy. Tech Trends, 39 (2), 22-24.

Mabrito, M. (1992): Computer-mediated communication and high-apprehensive writers : Rethinking the collaborative process. The Bulletin, 26-30.

Maccroff, G.I. (1988): The Empowerment of teachers : Overcoming the crisis of confidence. New Yourk : Teachers College Press.

Maier, P. et at (1998): Using Technology in Teaching and Learning, London: Koganpage.

McDaniel, E., McInerney, W. and Armstrong, P. (1992): Computers and School Reform. Educational Technology Research and Development, 41 (1), 73-78.

Means, B., and Olson, K. (1997): Technology and education reform: Washington, D.C. U.S. Department of Education.

MHRD (2000a): Sarva Shiksha Abhiyan (SSA)Guidelines, Govt. of India, New Delhi

MHRD (2000b): Sarva Shiksha Abhiyan : A programme for Universal Elementary Education. A framework for implementation, Govt. of India, New Delhi.

Mishra, S. (2005): Audio, Radio and Interactive Radio in Perspectives on distance Education: Educational Media in Asia, edited by Usha v. Reddi and Sanjay Mishra, Vancouver, Commonwealth of Learning, pp 71-78.

Mohanty, M.M. (2001): Empowerment of primary teachers and role of ICT: - Conceptual Analysis, in Report of International Workshop on Information and Communication Technology for Professional Development of Teachers, New Delhi, DEP-DPEP, IGNOU.

Moore, M.A., and Karabenick, S.A. (1992): The effects of computer communications on the reading and writing performance of fifth-grade students. Computers in Human behaviour, 8, 27-38.

Murnane, R. and Levy, F. (1996): Teaching the New Basic Skills: Principles for Educating Children to Thrive in a Changing Economy. The Free Press.

Naiman, D.W. (1988): Telecomunications and an interactive approach to literacy for disabled students. New York univ. (ERIC Document Reproduction Service No. ED 316 995)

NCERT (2000): Fifth Survey of Research in Education 1988-1993, Vol. I and II, New Delhi.

Neurath, P.(1966a): School Television in Delhi, All India Radio, Delhi.

Neurath, P.(1966b): School Television in Delhi, All India Radio, Delhi.

Newby, T., Stepich, D., Lehman, J., and Russel, J. (2000): Instructional technology for teaching and learning. Upper Saddle River, Merrill/Prentice hall, New Jerey.

Olaniran, B.A. (1994): Group performance in computer – mediated and face-to-face communication media. Management Communication Quarterly, 7 (3), 256-281.

Parkash, D. and Lal, H (1998): Using Satellite Technology for Special Orientation of Primary Teachers in Madhya Pradesh : A Study of Presentation and Production Values of Teleconferencing *Indian Journal of Open Learning*, 7(3), pp. 323-330.

Patel, I. (2000): Educational Telecasting in India : A Policy Perspectives in *Journal of Educational Planning and Administration* Vol. XIV, No. 4 (October, pp 345-357.

Planning Commission (1981): Sixth Five-Year Plan 1980-85, New Delhi Para 21.9, pp 353-354.

Radha Mohan (2004): Embedding Technology in Teacher Education – The Digital Edge in New Frontiers in Education ISSN: 0972-1231, Vol. XXXIV, No. 2, April-June 2004, pp. 147-152.

Rao, V.R. and Khan, Zeba (1997): Satellite-based Interactive Learning System. A Case Staff and *Educational Development International* 2 (1), pp 27-34.

Rao, V.R. and Khan, Zeba (1998): Satellite-based Interactive Learning System at IGNOU Retrospect and Prospects, A paper presented at International Conference on Collaborative Networked Learning, IGNOU, New Delhi, February 16-18, 1998.

Reddi, Usha V. (1996): Lessons from the Application of Communication Technology in Higher Education in India. In *Educational Technology,* 2000: A Global Vision of Open and Distance Learning Commonwealth of Learning (1997), Vancouver, BC, Canada.

Resta, P. (1996): Technology and changing views of the learning process. Texas School Boards Association Journal. 11 (8) Riel, M. (1994). Education change in a technology-rich environment. The Journal of Research on Computing in Education, 5, 261-274.

Riel, M. (2000): The future of technology and education : where are we heading? In Watson, D.M. and Downes, T. (Eds.) Communications and Networking in Education, Boston, MA: Kluwer Academic.

Ryser, G.R. Beeler, J.E., McKenzie, C.M. (1995): Effects of a computer-supported intentional learning environment (CSILE) on students' self-concept, self-regulatory behaviour, and critical thinking ability. Journal of Educational Computing Research, 13 (4), 375-385.

Sandholtz, J.H., Ringhstaff, C., Dwyer, D.C. (1997): Teaching with Technology: Creating student-centered classrooms. New York: Teachers College, Columbia University.

Senapaty, H.K. (2004): Integrating Digital Technology into Constructivist Learning Environment. Paper presented in the International Conference held at Saurastra University, Rajkot, Gujarat, India.

Shah, M.C. (1972): The Scope, Utility and Limitations of Educational Television in India, Ph.D., thesis M.S. University of Baroda, Gujarat.

Shukla, S. and Kumar, K. (1997): SITE Impact Study on Children, Ahmedabad, Space Applications Centre (mimeo).

Sudhish, M. (2005): Interactive Radio Instruction: Initiating for Change in tribal Schools of Chhattisgarh: A Case Study, Rajiv Gandhi Shiksha Mission, Raipur, Chhattisgarh.

Swan, K., and Mitrani, M. (1993): The changing nature of teaching and learning in computer-based classrooms. Journal of Research on Computing in Education, 26, 40.

Taleem Research Foundation (1999): Assessign the effectiveness f teleconferencing system of DEP-DPEP Programmes in Tamil Nadu, Ahmedabad.

Thomas, J. (2001): Audio for Distance Education and Open Learning: A Practical Guide for Planners and Producers, Vancouver and Cambridge, The Commonwealth of Learning and IEC.

Trivedi, Bela (1998): Network Utilization by User Agencies in Training and Development Communication Channel, Indian Space Research Organization, Ahmedabad, India.

UNESCO (2000a): Globalization and Living Together: Paris, The Challenges for Educational Content in Asia.

UNESCO (2000b): Information and Communication Technologies in Education; A Curriculum for Schools and Programmes of Teachers Development, Paris

UNESCO (2001): UNESCO Report: Teacher Education Through Distance Learning: Technology – Curriculum – Cost – Evaluation, UNESCO.

UNESCO (2002a): UNESCO Report: Information and Comunication Technologies in Teacher Education, A Planning Guide, Division of Higher Education, UNESCO

UNESCO (2002b): NESCO Report: Information and Communication Technology in Teacher Education, A Curriculum for Schools and Programme of Teacher Development. Division of Higher Education, UNESCO.

UNESCO (2002c): Information and Communication Technologies in Teacher Education – A Planning Guide, Paris.

Velayo, R.S. (1993): Cmputer conferencing as an instructional tool: exploring student perceptions of use, cognitive and motivational characteristics, and frequency of interaction (Cognition, motivation). Ph.D. Thesis, University of Michigan. Dissertation Abstracts AAC 9409831.

Vockell, E.L., and Schwartz, E.M. (1992): The computer in the classroom (Second Edition) New Yourk: Mitchell McGraw-Hill.

Vygotsky, Lev S. (1978): ind in Society: The Development of Higher Psychological Processes. Cambridge, MA: Harvard University Press.

Williams, A. (1995): Long-distance collaboration: A case study of science teaching and learning. In Spiegel, S.A., Collins, A., and Lappert, J. (Eds.), Action Research: Perspectives from Teachers' Classrooms. Southeastern Regional Vision for Education, 101-116.

Zucchermaglia, C. (1991): Toward a cognitive ergonomics of educational technology. Paper presented at the NATO Advanced Research Workshop on the Design of Constructivist Learning Environments, Leuven, Belgium.

❖ ❖ ❖

Index

❖ ❖ ❖